RIGHT-BRAINED POEMS FOR LEFT-BRAINED PEOPLE

Paul Jeffrey Davids

RIGHT-BRAINED POEMS FOR LEFT-BRAINED PEOPLE

First Edition Published by
Yellow Hat Publishing
A Division of Yellow Hat Productions, Inc.
5130 Neil Road Suite #430
Reno, Nevada 89502

First Printing, May 2012

The cover is a painting by the author entitled "Self-Portrait of Paul Davids in Paris" and is copyrighted 2011 by Paul Jeffrey Davids

ISBN 978-0-981-9244-5-8

I dedicate this book to my mother, Frances Davids, and my sister, Jeanie Anne Dwyer, who both express persistent enthusiasm for my poetry – and to my nephew Colin Dwyer, who excels in writing and literature, with emphasis on poetry. I also dedicate this book to Hollace G. Davids, my wife, who has been enthusiastic and supportive during all of my creative endeavors.

Foreword

They say the right brain is the center of inspired thinking that flows into the mind in creative bursts from dreams or as if from some ethereal realm, whereas the left brain is the center of logical thinking that structures the world into its perceived order and precision. I have friends who are artists who say they are "right-brained people." Accountants and engineers are often said to be "left-brained people." Of course, we don't have to be just one or the other – all of our brains have two hemispheres. However, sometimes one side or the other appears to be dominant.

I assume the poetry in this book originated in my right brain, but it has order and precision and deliberate, carefully structured rhyme that may be left brain characteristics. So in spite of the catchy title, these poems are really for everyone who has a brain (as long as you are willing to use it)!

My humorous poetry can be found in two books: POEMS TO READ WHILE DRIVING ON FREEWAYS (AND OTHER WAYS TO DIE LAUGHING) and also POEMS TO READ WHEN YOU RUN OUT OF WEED.

By contrast, this book is a collection of serious poetry that covers many themes. In the following pages you will find topics that range from fictional character tales to biographical/historic subjects to literary imagination and ruminations on life and death, and some conjectured purposes and meanings in human existence.

Some of the actual people in these poems (in addition to my father, Dr. Jules Davids) include Vincent van Gogh and Vincent's brother Theo, as well as Theo's murdered great grandson (also named Theo van Gogh); Edgar Allan Poe and his wealthy foster father, John Allan; the great film director/actor John Huston and his agent, Paul Kohner, who was known as "The Magician of Sunset Boulevard" and was my first employer in the entertainment business; Charles-Émil Reynaud, who I believe deserves to be acknowledged as the inventor of animation; Georges Méliès, the silent film director who was the subject of Martin Scorsese's film HUGO; Ray Harryhausen, the esteemed pioneer of special effects stop-motion with films such as THE 7TH VOYAGE OF SINBAD, JASON AND THE ARGONAUTS and the original CLASH OF THE TITANS; and Forrest J Ackerman, the scholarly but humorous original editor-in-chief of Famous Monsters of Filmland Magazine, who amassed a huge collection of science-fiction memorabilia over his long lifetime. He also insisted that a period never be used after his middle initial, so I have not used one.

The first poem in this collection, DON'T ASK A POET, actually rounded out the published collection of humorous poems, POEMS TO READ WHILE DRIVING ON FREEWAYS. I decided that's where I would begin this time, by repeating it here – it's reflective, and there is a certain irony in its tongue-in-cheek style that I would like those of you who don't have the other book to see.

In addition to the real people and historical personalities, you will meet some distinctive and memorable fictional characters in this collection, including Mistress Constance Clinghorn, the divorced schoolteacher who takes a final cruise at sea, and her dog, Ace, who has canine attitudes toward his self-destructive mistress; Harvard Hennesy, a successful, pot smoking intellectual who lost all sense of purpose in life because he never married the woman he loved; Aunt Tess, whose haunting of her nephew takes unexpected twists; Kate, who is a whore with a baby, desperate and abused; and John Hancock, who was born with the same name as the Revolutionary War icon, whose legacy inexplicably follows him around in his day to day life.

When I was an undergraduate at Princeton University, I was awarded the Morris B. Croll Poetry Prize (which was shared with another student, William Reginald Gibbons, whose work the judges liked very much too). The prize was for a free verse, lengthy poem called WADING IN A PHOTOGRAPH OF AUTUMN POND WATER. Although it differs in themes, mood, style and purpose from all the other works presented here, I have included it at the end as an example of my earliest poetic thoughts and efforts. (The only other free verse you'll find in this collection is in the two poems SOUL IN FLIGHT and THE DISSOLUTION OF UNBLEMISHED NATURE.)

The only problem with the poetry prize from Princeton was that some-how it seemed to end of my career as a poet before it began. Poetry seemed like such an arcane and impractical pursuit, I did not write any more poetry for several decades after winning the award. I do not really know why, except that I set out on a career in television and films as a producer/writer/director, as a novelist (Bantam published millions of copies of the six STAR WARS sequels I co-wrote with my wife, Hollace) and as a painter. In fact, I now have a large body of work as a painter, including the self-portrait on this cover.

Then a very unusual series of events began to occur in 2009 a few months following the passing of one of my mentors, Forrest J Ackerman (Forry). Suffice it to say, for the purposes of this Foreword, that those unusual events led me to begin an intensive study of the poetry of Edgar Allan Poe. I soon thereafter fractured my right ankle in a "freak accident" in our garden.

During my recuperation, and while unable to walk – and inspired by Poe's life and his poetry – I began writing poems from morning until night, day after day. Some were humorous, and some – those assembled in this collection – gave voice to some of my most serious reflections about life. The computer keys or the pen or pencil had to race to keep up with the words as they were forming almost effortlessly in my mind. My mother has asked repeatedly how it happened (the poetry, not the broken ankle), and my answer is: it is a mystery. But once it began, I would write these poems everywhere – not just when in front of a computer but also scrawled on scraps of paper wherever I happened to be.

The adage that truth is stranger than fiction has proven true for me time and again in my life. As of today, April 27th, 2012, I have written 84 poems since fracturing my ankle exactly 7 months ago. What follows are 28 of them, plus the poem from my days at Princeton.

I hope they will prove to be an enriching reading experience.

Table of Contents

1. DON'T ASK A POET

If facts you crave
On topics obscure
That few men appreciate
Or can endure

If scientific clarity
Is your only care
With precision quite perfect
Mathematics takes you there

And if knowledge arcane
From dusty centuries gone by
Calls out to you
Without making you sigh

And answers you need
That will never waver
Then listen well, my friend
I'll do you a favor

Don't ask a poet
Because a poet won't know it
No, don't ask a poet
Because a poet can't show it

And if you would build
An edifice tall
With elevators fast
And offices big and small

Or if you would design
A rocket for space
Don't ask a poet
A poet has no place

Nor should you consult a poet
If you will make a great ship
Or a train or a car
That needs no gas for a trip

Or if you want a faster computer
With a million gigabytes
Or a new modern city
With ten billion lights

Don't ask a poet
Because a poet can't hoe it
No, don't ask a poet
A poet would blow it

But if what you seek
Is ethereal, unseen
By all of the people
Who forgot how to dream

If you need inspiration
That comes from above
If you crave a new vision
That is filled with love

If artistic persuasion
Calls out to your heart
Then listen well, my friend
If you want to be smart

Go ask a poet
A poet will show it
Find yourself the best poet
A poet will know it

2. MY FATHER, JULES DAVIDS

A long life, it was not
Not long enough nearly
For a man of such intellect
Who saw the world clearly

His lips firm and straight
Easily offered a nice smile
His thick glasses so prominent
And there all the while

His part on the left
Somewhat receded
His gaze was far off
Small matters, unheeded

His forehead was large
Filled with deep thought
A serious demeanor
All his life, he taught

Georgetown University
He claimed as his home
School of Foreign Service
He wrote many a tome

A man for the centuries
Admired by all
His laughter was priceless
His embrace was for all

A husband and father
Devoted and true
He took time for his children
To impart what he knew

He grew up in Brooklyn
A ghetto through and through
His parents, Jewish immigrants
They spoke Yiddish too

The cafeteria, Brooklyn College
A place for discussions profound
For all the new students
Who gathered around

He met my mother
Spilling soup on her dress
No way to impress her
It made quite a mess

His bow-tie was proper
His features cut well
After college, marriage
All was well

I came along
Then my sister
Dad's mother died
Our grandma, we missed her

Dad gave up his cigarettes
For a white Meerschaum pipe
He typed on a manual
With a speed out of sight

His hobbies brought pleasure
Musician? He was not.
He played the piano
Mistakes? Quite a lot

In tennis he triumphed
Less than he would have liked
Swimming was essential
By day or by night

MY FATHER, JULES DAVIDS

His chess game was focused
He led with his knights
His golf always miniature
Lots of movies, quite right

Reading was his passion
Of books, there were many
He was fiscally frugal
Rarely wasting a penny

British comedy, his favorite
Peter Sellers was the best
Dad took me to movies
The good ones – and all the rest

TV sit-coms every night
California funnymen in turns
From Phil Silvers to Groucho
Jack Benny to George Burns

But the stuff of history
Was for Dad the sensation
Nothing escaped him
About our great nation

The whole story of America
Was his to command
How well he brought it to life
Behind a podium he would stand.

The students they loved him
His family did too
What a lantern of love
With a hole in his shoe

Like Adlai Stevenson
Whom he did adore
Humility ruled him
It reigned from his core

Paul Jeffrey Davids

My Dad – I do miss him
Life is just not the same
But I feel great joy
In just saying his name

The sound of his voice
The image of his face
His influence on me
No one will erase

A long life, it was not,
But he was loved dearly
A man of gentle wisdom
Who left us too early

This is my father's grave plaque at Mount Lebanon Cemetery in Hyattsville, Maryland.

Dr. Jules Davids teaching American Diplomatic History at Georgetown University (1950's). In the preface to John F. Kennedy's PROFILES IN COURAGE, *he is thanked for having "contributed materially to several chapters."*

3. WHAT SOME WISE MEN SAY

(*Note to the Reader:* This poem is about an epiphany. For me, that means a great and special moment when feelings suddenly transcend the here and now and make a great leap into a bigger perspective. Sometimes it means achieving a vast perspective in an instant. One suddenly feels one has a grasp on life, death, creation and eternity as if beholding it all from a distance. I often go to Big Bear Lake, California, and in a house on a street with no traffic lights, surrounded by a forest, one can see the stars and feel the forces of nature in ways that are impossible in a city. Closeness to nature in a calm, quiet and secluded moment is conducive to bringing about an epiphany. This is about one such moment and the thoughts it conveyed.)

Mighty musical sounds
Are all around
But the symphony
Perplexes me

This mountain so high
Pierces dark skies
The thunder prevails
And then it hails

Why am I here
To perceive so near
This moment of bliss
I would not miss?

Who created my ears
And my eyes and the light
The photons that strike
And bring me sight?

WHAT SOME WISE MEN SAY

Who fashioned the stone
On which I stand?
Who put me here
In this glorious land?

An accident
The pundits say
Just meaningless chance
Wending its way

Through a universe dark
Much colder than ice
A vast black void
A roll of the dice

But my mind rebels
Against answers without
Either love or glory
To my Maker I'll shout

You gave me life
You gave me sight
You gave me great gifts
And gave us all light

You created all love
The future you fashion
You gave us deep feelings
That spring from your passion

As hail turns to rain
Caressing the trees
So gentle and calm
There is a cool breeze

The night is approaching
The stars come alive
The moon is a sliver
Far beyond angry skies

We are helpless to know
Just why we are here
How did it all happen?
Is there knowledge we'll fear?

Do You have a face?
And a home we can see?
Do You exist all alone
In infinity?

Will we truly Awaken
As the dark turns to day?
Do You really care about us?
That's what some wise men say

4. LIKE A SNOWFLAKE

(*Note to the Reader:* Sometimes a poem will come to me while I'm a passenger in a car or at a restaurant. I'll jot it down quickly on a scrap of paper and cram it into my wallet or stick it in my pocket. I often think how I would feel if that scrap were to be lost. The poem would then be gone forever with no way to recapture it. That's because many times a poem is not a matter of calculation or deliberation built over time in layers that one might remember and reconstruct. Many of my poems are more like a very sudden and fleeting experience that comes in the flash of a moment and cannot be recaptured. That thought became the basis for this poem.)

A poem cannot be written twice
It comes like a snowflake on a wisp of ice
Not from the sky but from a cloud
Within the mind, declaring loud
Its message pure and so precise
A message crisp and quite concise
It comes just once in a flash of time
A thought transcendent and sublime
A few quick lines from pencil or pen
Take form like magic, and that is when
The thought does vanish from the mind
Gone forever, no matter how fine
Remaining only on that paper frail
Lose it and the words do fail
Ever to return in concept or form
Leaving the poet quite forlorn

5. THE CRUISE

Nowhere else had Constance cruised
Her soul was fragile, very bruised
Schoolteacher, she, of literature
But now no ailment could any book cure

She never ventured, that was her fate
Never journeyed on ocean nor river nor lake
This voyage, such a sad mistake
As if amends to her it could make

With spirits low, her dog in tow
She bit her lip and took a sip
As she read a poem of Edgar Poe
She loved Poe passionately – no, no, no!

The drink was coffee and a chaser of cognac
Her mastiff leaped up toward her warm lap
The booze warmed her trembling soul
Look, it was about to snap – that tall flagpole!

She fretted of course the wind's great force
How sad life had been since her divorce
The end of love, she had been betrayed
Into stormy feelings she did wade

She had thought of murder, once or twice,
Her ex-husband, Carl Clinghorn – cold as ice
She had dreamed of a dozen ways to kill
But then those thoughts had made her ill

In this state of mind, lost to time
She knew no better than to read those rhymes
Of that unsettling writer from long ago
That madman, Edgar Allan Poe

THE CRUISE

She turned a page, unsatisfied
And she was oh so horrified
That Poe, you know, was fit to throw
Overboard, what did he know?

Of life's true pleasures, Poe knew not
The sight of beauty he forgot
His mind was stark, his thoughts were dark
"This cruise," she sighed, "such a foolish lark"

The dog barked twice, nose cold and wet
"Nevermore," she declared with regret
With left hand holding her hat and hair
Kill her ex-husband? She didn't dare

But despise him – yes. Forget him – how?
It was time to act, and the moment was now
She took a deep breath, wishing it was her last
If she was going to do it, then she'd do it fast

"Nevermore will I go onto the deck
Wind and storms, I'm such a nervous wreck
To think such thoughts of life's cruel end
My spirit is fading, so a message I'll send
He'll know when the news he does hear
In pain he'll regurgitate all of his fear
That other woman whom he does prefer
Their passionate love I could not deter"

A few more lines she read with dismay
Why was she reading Poe's poems that day?
She was losing her mind at a rapid pace
And how was the makeup on her face?

She checked in a mirror, but the wind did blow
The mirror fell from her hand, and that angered her so
It cracked on the deck, such a small mirror too
What time was dinner? They'd be serving stew

That damned dog named Ace licked her face
She thought, "Nevermore will I plead Poe's case
I'm glad," she declared, "that his Lenore has died
For his lost Lenore, Poe never even cried"

"I hope," she said, "that he burns in hell"
And just at that moment a wave did swell
The top of that wave, white as a dove
Her heart ached so, for honestly – Poe she loved

But nevertheless, against him she raged
She glanced at her hands -- oh, how they'd aged
She said: "Nevermore will I read Poe's words
That raven was such a nasty bird"

Appalled was she at that awful word
Nasty – in her mind the word did disturb
Her tranquility, if such there be
But there was none, she was undone

"Did they bury Poe's bones in a hole quite deep?
I'll destroy this book, and then I'll sleep
Nevermore to accept the stain
Or feel the pain or sit in the rain
Oh, this miserable cruise, so filled with ennui
That dog of mine, I'm going to set him free"

She unfastened his leash and then his collar
How much did this cruise cost? Many a dollar
"Go," she said, "leave me alone
Go to the ship's kitchen, go beg for a bone"

But Ace stayed right there at her side
How the boat did toss, and not even high tide
Then Ace turned and across the deck did prowl
He glanced back at her, and he did growl

THE CRUISE

"Shut up, damned dog, jump off the deck!"
She glared at him, her nerves a wreck
And he stared right back but didn't choose
To acknowledge her or even move

"If only," said she, "some land I could see
For what I crave is victory
Over ocean or river or lake or sky
Right now! – Right now before I die!"

The rain pounded
The bells then sounded
Could she throw the book over the rail?
And that's when it began to hail

"I wish," she declared, "that nevermore
Will I find it necessary to deplore
The work of a writer of such fame
I hope to forget his very name
He dwells in evil and things so dark
His spirit is foul and very stark
But oh God do I wish he were still alive
For intercourse with him how I would strive
I'd kiss him boldly and copulate
But he's long dead, so we have no date
Forgive me, Ace, leaving you this way
Don't you have some toys? Go and play!"

Constance leaped overboard with a sudden turn
Hoping against hope that her soul would not burn
In hellfire fierce like the heart of the sun
Was there anything she had left undone?

Ace barked twice, trembling in his hide
Angry and tired of this infernal ride
Across ocean wide beneath sky so gray
On this cruise ship he just could not stay

By the rail he barked and then did moan
Why had she left him all alone?
How had she decided that her life must end?
Alone for himself now he would fend

He glanced at her book, all those pages blowing
Words and more words, everywhere showing
He understood not, nor did he care
Hearing her drown, he paused to stare

On all fours he lumbered toward the cabin warm
In his mind of a dog the thoughts did swarm
He'd find a new mistress, someone to lick
Or a bitch in heat, he still had a prick
His nails so sharp scratching hardwood floor
Entering the cabin, with his nose shut the door.
His Mistress Constance?
Insane to the core
His Mistress Constance?
Nevermore

6. HARVARD HENNESY

Harvard Henessey
Had nothing at all to do
When he awoke in the morning
The whole day was through

It was still a.m.
But he'd go back to bed
The pillows on his mattress
Were a perfect fit for his head

He wasn't lazy
And he certainly wasn't crazy
But he had come to the conclusion
Perhaps in a state of delusion
That life had no meaning
At least that's how it was seeming
To have no mission
Even when he went fishing
Which he seldom did
Because no one ever bid
Him to come along
No, his life was all wrong

And everything that he'd ever done
From honors bestowed and prizes won
To books written and countries visited
Including all the accolades he elicited
From Presidents and Heads of State
Honors he felt that came far too late
Had now led to a dreary spate
Of days in bed
Thinking of a girl he'd never wed
Janet Sue Sunnydale
Lost in time behind a misty veil

Perhaps if he could get off the couch
Then he could attest, yes he could vouch
For the fact that he once had been in love
With that lady sweeter than a dove

She had shared his life
And would have become his wife
But his time spent in intellectual pursuit
With royalties that brought him loot
And good old days so well spent
And so many honors heaven sent
And all his vast successes
All did presage
The lonely message
That the choice he made
To leave Janet Sue an old maid
Was a decision badly played

And after that choice was made
Harvard never again was laid
Nor did he ever deduce
That any effort to seduce
Another female
Would entail
An improvement to his life
Though he still had no wife

The problem wasn't one of sex
The issue was that there was a hex
Upon his spirit which had sunk so low
Because in his heart he did know
That one day all life on Earth would end
The sun would explode and that would send
Our planet hurling, turning into ash
And perhaps into Mars the Earth would crash
And all of human hopes and dreams
No matter how safe everything now seems
Would evaporate in a puff of smoke
Which reminded him to take a toke

HARVARD HENNESY

He liked to toke on a little weed
His dealer's prices showed such greed
Expensive stuff, that drug called grass
He thought whoever outlawed it was an ass
And although marijuana did calm him down
The Devil's weed also spun him around
And the higher and higher his mind did go
Then with more certainty did he know
That the end of the world was coming soon
Perhaps even before spring would bloom

So what was the use in getting out of bed?
Considering where man's ignorance had led
To planetary destruction on a cosmic scale
Killing off so many species, even the whale

When the alarm clock rang
He never sprang
Up from the bed
No, he felt dead
He had no pep
He had no zest
His state of depression
Was at a crest

But Harvard was quite able
To reach the dining room table
Usually to himself he was talking
While undertaking the task of walking
To the shelf with his books
Where a visitor looks
To see his publications
From various nations

It made him so weary
All of life was dreary
And there was nothing to do
Had he put on a shoe?

No, he had not
Look at where he'd got
He had not even a sock
Life was a crock
Of nonsense and more
He shuffled to the door
Of the very fine kitchen
Thinking of fetchin'
A little weed
That would quench his need
Then something to eat
But he felt beat
And there was no hunger or thirst
That part was the worst

If only he had wanted to eat
Or sit in his comfortable seat
Or look out the window and stare
Without going anywhere
But none of that was pleasing
He reached up to a shelf, seizing
His bag of strong weed
And not a single marijuana seed
Cluttered the perfection
Of that wild confection

He took a puff
And all the stuff
In the room all around
Started making sounds
The door, it creaked
The faucet leaked
Then colors grew bright
A psychedelic sight

He dropped into a soft chair
And ran a hand through his hair
What was left of his hair
Yes, people would often stare

HARVARD HENNESY

Because once his hair long
Had made him look strong
But now most was lost
To his pride, quite a cost

Oh, how he sighed
With the pot pipe at his side
Perhaps he nearly cried
Something deep inside had died!

He should have been quite happy
But his spirit was so sappy
Because it was a fact he did fail
Ever to wed Janet Sue Sunnydale

Oh, where was she now?
Could he find out somehow?
Or was she lost to all time?
Someone he'd never find?

Perhaps she'd had a date
With some man who'd become her mate
Perhaps her name was new
The thought made Harvard blue

But perhaps bells never did jingle
Perhaps Janet Sue was still single
Perhaps still with a beautiful face
Did she still live in the same place?

The years that had passed
Since that time when last
They had been together
In such fine weather
In the spring of their days
Now surrounded him with haze

For her he did long
He had surely done wrong
Their best days were gone
And what was their song?

He couldn't remember
Why couldn't he remember?
It was something about September
And love's last fading ember

Were these recollections futile?
No, no! He'd try Google
To find Janet Sue
That should do

But he could not get up
He was quite stuck
He legs rebelled
Feeling totally repelled
About the idea of lifting
This sad man who was sifting
Through memories lost
At an emotional cost

He saw his computer
So far away
At least ten feet, he'd say
Would it take him all day?
To rise and stoop low
To boot it up, make it go
Better to sleep
And perhaps there he'd meet
Janet Sue Sunnydale in a dream
They'd be together, it would seem

But at very long last
To his computer he went
All his strength was sapped
Enthusiasm, quite spent

At the screen he stared
While a search he did make
Success came quickly
Could it be a mistake?

There was her name
But more than one
He wondered: in all those years
What had she done?

Once she had been an actress
On the stage now and then
And one name on the list
Had done theater when
This very year had begun
Ahah! Her new theater troupe
Was a community group

And then on a listing
That was near the top
Was the address for her email
His jaw did drop
In amazement and sorrow
Well, he'd write her tomorrow
Yes, he'd send an email
But perhaps it would fail
To receive a reply
And then by and by
His time would come
Without seeing her again
...He would die

That thought gave him traction
He was stirred into action
He was indeed quite a sight
As he began to write

He searched for the right words
That would somehow explain
That his obsession with career
Had been entirely lame

He wanted to say
Not in an awkward way
That he thought about her often
Could he admit every day?

How could he bridge the gap
Of years fallen away?
How could he reach out to her
In a special way?

Suddenly he knew
Yes, he knew just what to do
He wrote: Hi Janet, it's Harvard
I'm fine, how are you?

It was a start
But not enough heart
What else to add
Without sounding sad?

Janet, my life
Took a turn in its track
When we said goodbye
There was no turning back
But if only I could
Now turn back the clock
I would tell you I loved you
Is that a big shock?

No email reply
Popped into his in-box
So he spent his days studying
The value of his stocks

Week followed week
He soon felt like a geek
His heart felt an ache
Was writing to her a mistake?

The silence was awful
The lack of reply brought dread
He decided things would get better
If he went back to bed

He sent that email again
And then once more
And then one dreary day
A surprise was in store

For into his in-box
Came the awaited email
Yes, that one was from
Janet Sue Sunnydale

What did she say in it?
He'd find out in a minute
His heart it did flutter
His words came in a stutter

He opened the email
His eyes read and re-read
Every word in her missive
Every word that she said

It said: Hi Harvard, it's Janet
I'm glad that you're fine
I think of you too
From time to time
We ought to get together
If you come this way
I've got a bottle of wine
That I'll save for that day

That day finally arrived
When they opened the wine
It was a day to remember
When his spirit felt fine

It was like beginning anew
Recapturing when they were young
And remembering that old song
They once had sung

7. THEO AND THEO

(*Note to the Reader:* This poem deals with the tragedy not only of the life of Vincent van Gogh, but his brother Theo, and Theo's great grandson, also named Theo van Gogh, who was murdered by an Islamic extremist in Holland in 2004. It draws parallels in family tragedies that span centuries. The idea for it came to me while I was in Paris, walking in the neighborhood near the Moulin Rouge, looking for the apartment where Theo van Gogh lived during the final decade of his brother Vincent's life, which ended in 1890. There, in that one apartment, at that time the majority of all Vincent van Gogh's paintings were stored, some rolled up, others on wooden stretchers. In those days, Theo was an art dealer and supported his brother, a failed artist whose work could not be sold, for there were no buyers. Theo sensed that there was worth in his brother's work. But no man then alive could have supposed that within 100 years, the canvases that had been stored in that one apartment would be appraised by world-wide art museums at somewhere between one to two billion dollars. I found the apartment, and with my wife, Hollace, alongside me, we stared up at its windows with reverence and awe.)

The tireless measure of chiming clocks
Scarcely hint at the scars of the century past
And from the Moulin Rouge, how many blocks?
So many questions remain unasked

My steps unsure as I plod and then stop
Beneath the glorious hill of famed Montmartre
Home of cemeteries with famous plots
Yet lacking the bones of Jean Paul Sartre

Above me at hilltop
The white marble domes
Claim the high ground
While narrow streets I comb

The Sacré Coeur looms
Higher than many birds fly
Reminding me of the tombs
Of saints who die

My thoughts are not of heaven
Nor of amusements profane
My mind traverses a century
To some of Vincent's bitter days

I arrive near apartment fifty-four
The windows have flowers quaint
Rue Lepic reads the sign near door
Filled with awe, I feel faint

Behind those window
More than a century ago
Were hundreds of paintings
By Vincent van Gogh

Theo and Johanna's home
Proper and smart
Upright and stable
Theo dealt in fine art

He was Vincent's younger brother
By four years
For his brother's paintings
Friends offered sneers

In an era when realism
Was the artist's measure
In Vincent's vision
The world took no pleasure

Vincent who had failed once and again
Art salesman he was not, nor preacher then
Brushes and pallet were all Vincent knew
Wild invention with color's strongest hue

THEO AND THEO

That world condemned poor Vincent's work
But in Theo's heart did passion lurk
For canvases to which Vincent gave birth
Like a whirling dervish leaping from the Earth

Theo alone was there
To stand by his older brother's side
Theo's money
Paid for the wild ride

And now of people who are
Both large and small
For me Theo van Gogh
Hovers over all

What courage that man
Forever displayed
And for that courage
A large price he paid

Their father barred Vincent
From the family home
Disapproving, unmoving
Gave neither funds nor loan

Theo's mercy and love
And admiration
Sustained Vincent's life
Brought animation

Johanna agreed, standing at Theo's side
One day there might be a change of tide
But in the 1880's there was a firm verdict
For galleries Vincent's work would not be picked

To hang in galleries or even homes
Impossible, Vincent stood all alone
But in his brother's apartment small
In piles high Theo accepted them all

Every month Theo paid Vincent's rent
And for food and paints the money was sent
To a yellow house in Arles Vincent was leasing
Theo's conviction, it was unceasing

To Theo's apartment at fifty-four
Vincent's paintings arrived by this very door
This Rue Lepic did gloriously crown
A treasure for the world, without a sound

No applause or shouts
Nor celebrations merry
For that collection so bold.
Brilliant colors? Very!
And starry nights
And irises blooming
By fields of wheat
Where crows were looming

As I contemplate the grandeur of belief
How it feeds the soul, how it brings relief
The mysterious expanse of inner knowing
Conviction that leaves the spirit glowing
And artistic grandeur ever upward inching
My very cheek I now am pinching
To be sure my feet have brought me here
To this hallowed ground I hold so dear

Vincent's sinking spiral is known so well
His life descending into a morass of hell
Without Theo's devotion, steadfast and true
What was Vincent ever to do?

Vincent's ear half-severed, his sanity in flight
Theo and Johanna sensed the onset of night
And when Vincent his life did tear asunder
Theo trembled, it was like thunder

THEO AND THEO

Like the crest of a river in the pale of time
I sail over those days and that very hour
In his respectable clothes, pressed and fine
Theo enters Vincent's room, heartsick and dower

"My brother dear, Vincent
What have you done?
Your wound is fatal
And nothing has been won
By your impending death
A horrifying loss
To this world of ours
Such a bitter cost"

"My dear brother, Theo
I'll love you forever
Your faith in me
Has deserted me never
For one such as me
Forty years are many
And before you impart to me
Every last penny
This is my wish
May you and Johanna make it so
Help this sorry world
To awaken and to know
That there was some artistic worth in me
With that I know you surely agree."

He took his last breath, his head fell to the sheet
His poor brother Theo clutched his trembling seat
And glanced around that small room one last time
There was one final painting, a swift blur out of mind

A wheatfield with crows scattering in dark sky
Where would dear Vincent's shattered body lie?
A suicide in that era, unholy don't you see?
No room at church cemeteries for blasphemy

Barely five months later, Theo's poor heart failed
A cruel, sudden disease his health assailed
Vincent's body, moved near a church he painted
Theo's ashes buried alongside, memories untainted

A few decades then passed
After Vincent and Theo's lives extinguished
It was Johanna who then proved herself
Immensely distinguished

She revealed letters to Theo
That Vincent did write
The whole story of Vincent
At last came to light
She cried out to Paris
City of their souls
Challenging the conscience
As if with hot coals

"Look at these works
What faults do you see
In Vincent our genius
Whose soul is now set free?
These paintings so bright
Do shine light from above
On the miracle of life
And the lands that we love."

And little by little
Step by slow step
Those who cried no tears
Those who never wept
For the artist whose earlobe
Was sliced away
Woke up to discover
Who had left them that day

His work endeared many
In the decades to come
The heart of the art world
Unquestionably won

Remorse and regret
For a hero barely known
Respect and admiration
Were the new tone

Without Theo
Who lovingly supported his brother
Without Theo
Whose dedication was like that of a lover
There would be no Sunflowers
Nor Irises nor Night Cafe
And the entire collection
Would have withered away

So Theo you are surely
A great light to admire
And for your children
And all that should someday transpire
Are there blessings awaiting
That redeem this existence?
Will your generations to come
Inherit your persistence?

Fifty-six years
After Theo van Gogh died
Another Theo van Gogh
Was born with talent and pride
In Amsterdam
Home of his family long passed
He entered this world
Intending to last

A world knowing and growing
With technology advanced
Cinema now existed
A new circumstance

Instead of canvases of oil
Made with brushes and toil
Motion pictures enticed him
Like fresh fertile soil

This man was the great grandson
Of poor Vincent's brother
A sharp eye for the camera
And themes like none other

With memories keen
Of Grandma Johanna's achievement
For oppressed women of the world
He felt bereavement

His eye turned to controversy
Islam and the female
And with camera and film
He conveyed quite a tale

He called his film SUBMISSION
Provoking anger profound
And much resentment
From the Muslims around

Religious sanction of oppression
That was Theo's theme
Liberation versus domination
What did it all mean?

Brash and combative
That was this Theo's stance
He became a target of jihad
Attracting the lance

THEO AND THEO

One morning in two thousand four
Theo holding handlebars, riding his bike
While his killer with handgun
Approached the man he disliked

Mohammed Bouyeri
Murdered Theo van Gogh
In broad daylight in Amsterdam
The land Theo's family did know

He shot him eight times in the chest
Then pulled out the knife
And not content with the deed
Of merely taking that life
A second knife too
For attacking the dead
He did his utmost
To cut off Theo's head
One knife into the body
To attach a note of five pages
No matter what Theo achieved in life
These were his wages
The note it rambled on
With all sorts of news
Hatred of the west
And especially the Jews

So this is where it led
Great grandfather's love
Whose brother's treasures
Were like gifts from above

Can someone explain
This perverse twist of fate?
Is redemption for mankind
Simply too late?

In the Vatican now
Though Vincent so sinned
One of his paintings is on display
THE PIETA, quite grim

The dead tortured body
Of Christ without tears
Four million people
Saw it last year

This is a pen-and-ink drawing I made of a Paris street that I passed en route to Theo's apartment.

In my adventurous days as a young man in Paris (when I participated in the Summer Work Abroad Program of Princeton University), I worked as a translator and then as a camera salesman in Au Printemps Department Store. I'm at the left, toasting with coffee cups with Parisian friends.

I was a young artist in Paris while part of the Princeton Summer Work Abroad Program.

I wrote, produced and directed STARRY NIGHT, a feature film fantasy about Vincent van Gogh returning to Earth for 100 days in our time. Hollace Davids also produced. Distributed by Universal Home Entertainment and Universal Television.

8. LIFE

Of mysteries big and conundrums small
There are two things that transcend them all
From where does life come and where does it go?
That is the challenge we seek to know

There is in the beginning one first breath
And in the end at the time of death
An exhalation final and long
Erasing recollection of all we do wrong

We are made of cells, each one distinct
Each cell has a function quite unique
And if our powers were not so weak
Then beyond the veil we all could peek

Some claim to hold the mysterious key
That brings the light that a few can see
They spout the answers in church or temple
Tell me, can it really be that simple?

Of possibilities as vast as the well of time
Some believe that we all emerged from slime
From chaos cruel or harmonies kind
Somehow there arose the human mind

With perceptions defined by senses five
We declare that we are indeed alive
Our vision confined by the spectrum of the eye
And no man or woman can ever explain why

The scents of cheese or apple pie
Have no beholder when we die
The sense of touch, a compelling tingle
Urges us to mate and mingle

Courage forces us all things to dare
While the ears capture vibrations in the air
Our blood flows ceaselessly within
On males of age, a bearded chin

Our lips do seek a splendid potion
While our legs enact every motion
Our hearts while beating cause commotion
And do convey every range of emotion

We love, we hate
We destroy, we create
We battle and war
Win or lose, we keep score
Wrongdoers we seldom excuse
But with free will we can surely choose
To forgive or despair
To rest indifferent – or care

Someone with infinite persistence
Did surely will life into existence
Perhaps that's false – or perhaps it's true
I haven't got a clue – have you?

9. DEATH

Our stake in immortality
Is rather like a stately tree
Leaves shrivel and crumble, like teeth and nails
In winter's hail, new growth -- it fails
Dormant in snow, ever sleeping
Awaiting the seasons of growth and reaping
The branches bare, like our limbs in death
While the great trunk defies time's mighty breath

In winter, where resides the life of a tree?
New leaves in spring, how can this be?
The corpse decays and returns to earth
Will someday there come another birth?
The soul ascends and comprehends
The heart resolves and life's hurts do mend

Therefore, never in all this whole world wide
Is there a man or woman who really died
And all the tears that are cried each day
Beside coffins where tired bodies lay
Are surely in vain, unleashed by tension
Because those in grief lack comprehension
That a soul exists beyond the physical
And that the truth is really quite mystical
And the realms beyond are not just mythical
The plan of life has parts invisible

10. HERE LIES EDGAR ALLAN POE

Earlier in this collection, the poem THE CRUISE was about Constance Clinghorn, a divorced lady school teacher aboard a cruise ship, reading a book of works by Poe as she contemplates her life. It may be out of the ordinary in a book of poetry to include a chapter of prose, however, since two poems about the life of Edgar Allan Poe follow this chapter (JOHN ALLAN and THE POE HOUSE IN BALTIMORE) and two other poems later on in this book also involve Poe (BY THE LIGHT OF A STAR and the fiction horror poem EDGAR, THE INTRUDER), I have included a brief biography to prime my reader for the continuing Poe poetic experience. This is a slightly revised version of an article I wrote that was originally published in the magazine Famous Monsters of Filmland (#260) under the expanded title: HERE LIES EDGAR ALLAN POE, MASTER OF MAYHEM AND THE MACABRE.

Edgar Allan Poe, dark lord of literary horror, hoax and mystery, was born in a Boston rooming house in a frigid January in 1809, and he departed this earth in Baltimore 24 days before Halloween in 1849, a lifetime of only about 40 years. Since young Edgar began writing while still in grade school, he accomplished all of his works in approximately 30 years: about 64 poems, some of considerable length, and about 70 short stories. There was one work considered a novel (THE NARRATIVE OF ARTHUR GORDON PYM OF NANTUCKET) and a very long piece he referred to as a prose poem called EUREKA. It was his attempt to describe the universe, physics, metaphysics and all of cosmology and astronomy, including proposing something akin to the Big Bang Theory as the point of origin of all creation.

However, he was also a ferocious critic, usually writing for magazines. If you were a novelist or poet famous in that era, you might have hoped to go unnoticed by Poe (unlikely). That's because whether you were Keats or Shelley or Coleridge or Longfellow or Dickens or any other of the literary gods of that time who are now worshipped in college English departments today, Poe would surely find fault with your writing. And a lot of those literary icons didn't much care for him – except in France, where he became one of the only American literary heroes, way before anyone much cared about him in the United States. He struggled, he scraped, he stewed, he was betrayed, he was scorned, court-martialed, fired repeatedly, knew frequent heartbreak, and he lived through every type of financial deprivation and health catastrophe.

Climb into his shoes. Let's pretend you are Edgar Allan Poe. This is your life.

You were born in Massachusetts into a world without airplanes, where the steam engine would come to rule. It was a world without cars or world wars. You are destined to die four years before Vincent van Gogh will be born (another artist who suffered mightily and was also widely scorned).

You found yourself in an America that still had slaves. Though born in the north, you spent most of your early life in the south and became a southern gentleman. Slavery never troubled you. Your sympathies, as an adult, were not with the abolitionists, but that was somehow natural considering the traditions of the Old South.

You were born into a world that had never known science-fiction or detective mystery stories, almost a century before silent movies would be invented. As for science-fiction, you would invent it – and Jules Verne and H. G. Wells would owe much to you. As for detective mystery stories, you would invent those too. Sir Arthur Conan Doyle would forever be in your debt. Would there ever have been a Sherlock Holmes without your French detective Dupin preceding him?

Of course, horror stories would become your greatest legacy, along with vivid poetry, some of it horrific in its own way, such as THE RAVEN. Today every schoolchild has read or memorized the opening lines of THE RAVEN. "*Once upon a midnight dreary, while I pondered weak and weary, over many a quaint and curious volume of forgotten lore.*" Along came a raven who, tapping and rapping and nearly catching you napping, said one word and one word only: "*Nevermore.*" And somehow that one word assured that after years of toiling without fame or glory, that now you would be unknown nevermore.

But no riches came from THE RAVEN, the basis for many modern films. Some say you received nine dollars for it. Others say fifteen. The bottom line is, there were no reprint rights, no royalties, no sequel and prequel payments: You were ripped off. Dying about a century before independent film producer Roger Corman came along had its disadvantages. If you had survived until today, you would probably own your own Hollywood studio.

But never mind the poverty for a moment. You would prove again and again what a romantic heart you had. Your poetry is rich with imagery about beautiful women who died young (LENORE). And so many of the women in your life, from your own mother to your young wife, Virginia (your cousin, who passed away in her 20's), would die young.

Your mother, Elizabeth Poe, was a much-loved, beautiful stage actress. You inherited her dramatic talent in your vivid imagination, and you also inherited your sense of story and verbal rhythm and poetry.

Your father, David Poe, Jr., was an actor who never received good reviews, who couldn't stand in your mother's shadow as a performer, and who took up drinking and deserted your mother and you.

Your mother's death from illness when you were three years old threw your childhood existence into turmoil.

Fortunately (or unfortunately, depending upon how one ultimately keeps score), you were swiftly taken into a well-to-do southern home. You became the foster son of the Allan family of the state of Virginia. John and Frances Allan were like your parents for the next fifteen years or so, but they never adopted you. Eventually John Allan caused as much damage in your existence as the desertion of your father.

The psychological scars John Allan inflicted on you, after behaving as a loving parent for many years, sentenced you to a life of economic hardship when he easily could have given you a life of comfort and plenty. He became one of the richest men in Virginia, but there came a day when he would not give you one more dollar.

However, before you were cut off from the Allan fortune and forced to make your way in the world with no help at all, there were some good years of childhood. And John Allan spoiled you as a child. He gave you everything you wanted and more.

The Allans knew you had many talents. You excelled at almost everything you attempted. You were an athlete. You outshined all your friends in athletics and even took up arduous physical challenges including long distance swimming. In school, you distinguished yourself. When the well-to-do Allan family moved to England for several years, as John Allan attempted to expand his corporation's business to Europe, the teachers quickly had you pegged as their favorite. You read so much and mastered the meaning and intent of much literature. The town in Scotland where you lived (where John Allan was born) was also the town of writer Daniel Defoe, who wrote Robinson Crusoe about one century before you were born. How you loved that book! And how many times you read it! It helped you as a writer, teaching you precision and writing with detailed description.

Your foster father was proud of you then, for a brief time.

What happened to turn your relationship with him into a disaster?

If only you had remained true to him, and he to you, but that wasn't destined to be. When John Allan came into his inheritance from his uncle, making him incredibly rich, your future security could have been assured if you hadn't done everything you could think of to spoil it.

You had strong self knowledge and you revealed, in one of your short stories, what your principle problem was in life. That story was called THE IMP OF THE PERVERSE. It was about how people can be the source of their own undoing. It told how there is a little imp in the brain which dares us again and again to go against our better judgment. An imp that makes us take horrible risks. An imp who convinces us to push every situation in life into something dangerous and self-destructive. And that described you perfectly. You allowed your imp of the perverse to rule you. And part of the problem was alcohol.

When John Allan sent you to college, you drank and gambled. You were a miserable gambler, and John Allan resented having to clean up your gambling debts.

After one semester, he stopped paying for you to go to the university (where old Thomas Jefferson had once shown up personally). Your only choice then was to join the army. And when you self-published a first book of poems and could no longer tolerate being an enlisted man, you appealed to John Allan for help. He ignored you. He didn't even write you to tell you that your foster mother, Frances Allan, was deathly ill.

After Frances died, John Allan reconciled with you briefly. He supported your effort to gain an appointment to the U.S. military academy at West Point.

That also turned to disaster, when you decided to do everything in your power to get yourself court-martialed.

No one can see the future. But in spite of your own personal imp of the perverse, you somehow were entirely confident of your eventual success. Your first book of self-published poems is very rare today. One single copy has sold at auction for over $600,000.

You were determined to be the first American writer to support himself entirely with writing. But there were so many things going against you. There were no copyright laws protecting European writers, so why would American publishers want to publish your work when they could publish Charles Dickens for free? You gradually worked your way onto the staff of the Southern Literary Messenger as assistant editor. They published and helped place some of your early stories. With a small salary, you even secretly married your thirteen year old cousin, Virginia, whom you deeply loved. You both lied about her age on the marriage certificate. And then you were fired for drinking.

However, no matter what the disaster in your personal life, you always kept writing. In your day, some suspected you of living an immoral life, of being a drug addict, or being sinister and perverse. The truth was rather different, though. You were a gentleman, handsome and polished and charming and even sweet for the ladies, a captivating public speaker, some said considerate and somewhat modest. It was only your imagination that was dark, and there you knew a world without limits. The horrors of your black cat whose eye one of your characters sliced out, the terror of the old man with the roaming eye whose heart kept beating after death (beneath the floorboards), the nightmare of the pendulum that would slice a prisoner in half as he was chained in the pit – or the premature burials and those who awoke from death – even the Masque of Red Death itself.... they all had a dark and macabre existence in your mind and on your pages. You live today in the public imagination because no one else could delve into horror the way you did. As for your literary skill, it is debated still. Mark Twain thought your writing was mediocre and dull. Beaudelaire, who translated your works into French and wrote introductions, thought you were a literary genius of the highest order.

The circumstances of your death remain an unsolved mystery. Some still suspect foul play. There is a theory that the angry brothers of your childhood sweetheart (to whom you unsuccessfully proposed marriage) beat you up, forced you to drink a lethal amount of alcohol, and left you for dead in a Baltimore alley. No one can explain how you were found wearing clothes not your own, or what you meant as you stammered incoherently for a few hours before you passed away. But regardless of the cause of your death, or the fact that only a handful of mourners showed up when you were buried, there are many who now worship you as a literary god. Your gift of literary treasures has endured.

Now come two of my poems that vivify your life and legacy: JOHN ALLAN, which explores your tragic relationship with your foster father, and THE POE HOUSE IN BALTIMORE, which considers the fate of the house in which you once lived with your aunt Clemm and your cousin, Virginia, who became your wife.

11. JOHN ALLAN

More than a hundred sixty years gone by,
Since John Allan's foster son did die
Found in a gutter in Baltimore
In the buttoned up black coat he always wore

He was in quite a stupor, rum and laudanum
And no one knew where he'd come from
For one week before he could not be found
His mental state, quite unsound

If time could be twisted and lived again
Should we change any one day back then?
For if one thread unraveled the weave
Those gifts of his pen, would we still receive?

The words of the master, just like fine wine
Immortal themes from out of time
Brilliance with a perfect flourish
Our inward lives young Poe did nourish

But John Allan, I rage against you still
Exhibit "A" of course is your will
Your reckoning has waited far too long
Can you finally confess to a life gone wrong?

Your wife Frances had a heart of gold
Childless yes, but what did unfold?
Your home had not a single toy
Until you received a three year old boy

His journey from birth, it was not fair
Young Edgar, entrusted to your care
His father David fled in the night
Leaving wife and children, it was not right

But let us turn back one more page
Edgar's mother Eliza, beauty of the stage
She loved her little Edgar so,
Then came consumption, the rest you know

Orphaned at three, nowhere to turn
Edgar came to your home, his need did burn
He became your foster son, none other
Your wife Frances, how she wanted to mother

For awhile your heart was truly glad
A family united was what you had
Proud you were of this fine foster son
Who excelled, leaving no great deed undone

Whether leadership or sports or speech
To Edgar Poe you had much to teach
His tutors were all amazed, recall
This boy so quickly learned it all

Fine English poems the boy soon read
Charming lad is what his tutors said
Perfect recitations and a musical ear
Your foster son was near and dear

The business flourished, or so you thought
A new branch in England was what they bought
With tickets purchased at quite a fee
Thirty-four days crossing the Atlantic sea

The village you chose proved quite a show
A hundred years before, Daniel Defoe
Had lived right there, his spirit hovered
And from his book, Edgar never recovered

ROBINSON CRUSOE he read once and again
And not long thereafter Edgar took up his pen
Gazing into the future, seeing nothing to fear
Now filled with fervor for a literary career

JOHN ALLAN

A very fine boy, and quite a fine scholar
Those were your words, and you spared him no dollar
Spoiled they said, of young Edgar Poe
But he was your boy then, and how could you know?

Your business would suffer, the income would slide
Far away in America, it came out of your hide
You transplanted your family back home one and all
A struggle awaited, but no time for a fall

I try to fathom the paths you both took
Your head on business, your son's mind in a book
And then that crucial year, eighteen twenty-five
Your immensely rich uncle was no longer alive

William Galt passed away at your breakfast table
His wealth was profound, and it was no fable
A million dollars or more, he bequeathed to you
Now surrounded by wealth, what did you do?

Bought a great stately mansion
Huge Virginia columns
Slaves and gardens
A life quite solemn
Comfort and luxury
Never a care
But Edgar Poe
You could no longer bear

Adopt your foster son?
Officially no.
Give him your name?
His name would stay Poe

Send him to college?
Well just for a year
He gambled and drank
For him not a tear

Was it his fault, having a troubled soul?
Did he ever abandon his lifelong goal?
A few poems he published, his spirit not shattered
Didn't you teach him that literature mattered?

You paid his few debts, then denied him a penny
You spent on your affairs, they say there were many
Your jealousy burned, you were so unjust
From your great lavish home, this lad was thrust

And all the while, you cheated on your wife
And soon Frances was ill, in fear of her life
For Edgar the army was his only hope
A struggle eternal for the writer to cope

Did he really deserve this forced life apart
Didn't he write to you, seeking your heart?
And how many replies to your foster son?
History tells us: only one

He approached you sincerely, stirring up zeal
Almost forced to his knees, he made his appeal
With your power and influence, you could try to appoint
Edgar Poe as a cadet at West Point

Like Edgar, you drank, got your nose out of joint
No problem for you if Edgar went to West Point
Of course there was a little money to pay
You came up with that money in a year and a day

Did you even care, when your wife finally died?
How many months before you took a new bride?
A much younger woman, you were fifty-one
You had fond hopes Louisa would bear you a son

Edgar's heart sank as you began your new life
He foretold many more days of strife
For him West Point did not really suit
He sought a court-martial, they gave him the boot

JOHN ALLAN

Then came your letter, so final and firm:
"Don't write to me Edgar – you are a worm
And don't ever seek my mind to deceive
Not one word from me is what you'll receive"

You were soon fifty-four, Louisa gave you two sons
And a baby girl, too, so your old life was done
Eighteen thirty-four, illness came in a flurry
One day to the next, you were gone in a hurry

At long last, John Allan, you were dead
They unveiled the will, and it was read
Suspense gripped fair Edgar, waiting to know
If you'd chosen to grace him or lay him low

The estate was a fortune
Poe was poor beyond hope
Surely you could have at least
Left him some rope

Of the estate with its riches
None went to him
Cruel-hearted John Allan
That was your sin

The story's well known
Of Edgar's next years
There were only fifteen of them
And then came the tears
Not many were shed
For that genius so rare
So many lies told
About his dark lair

Three hundred fifty's the number
That saw the light
Of the stories and poems
That he did write

He spent a lifetime in poverty
Seeking food and coal
A young wife he loved
God bless her poor soul

Virginia died young
With no blanket or shawl
Edgar's heart died with her
That's the truth of it all

He saw fame but not fortune
Popularity strong
Some admired his insight
But he sang a strange song

Sherlock Holmes would not exist
Were it not for Poe
The detective story?
Poe invented the show

This is the original Edgar Allan Poe Postage Stamp.

This is the Edgar Allan Poe Commemorative Stamp.

H. G. Wells and Jules Verne?
Is science fiction what you admire?
Poe invented that too
His imagination was on fire

And if horror and terror
Are your cup of tea
Without Poe they are nothing,
Don't you all see?

And so heartless John Allan
If I could change your will
I wonder what of Poe's legacy
Would be with us still?

If a rich man he'd been
With luxury too
Would he have ended up
Forgotten, like you?

Edgar Allan Poe (1809 - 1849)

12. THE POE HOUSE IN BALTIMORE

(*Note to the Reader*: Another true tale, this one based on the possible demise, for financial reasons, of the Edgar Allan Poe museum at a home where Poe lived in Baltimore. The 203 Amity Street museum accepts donations to try to persevere, now that the city has terminated its subsidy. The city of Baltimore maintains its annual subsidy for the Babe Ruth home and museum, but the Poe Museum, like the Sir Arthur Conan Doyle home in London, has had a hard time maintaining its sources of official support. "Fringe" writers, no matter how famous and immortal, do not appear to have a level of prestige equal to a famous baseball player.)

The house Edgar Allan Poe lived in on Amity Street in Baltimore

Edgar Poe, pity Baltimore
Your city has now shut the door
On your home on Amity Street
Remembrance – Nevermore!

The old Amity house
Has attained quite a station
Amity means friendship
Peace for this nation

Refuge you found there
A hundred sixty years ago
The brick house now under siege
From a financial foe

THE POE HOUSE IN BALTIMORE

A museum it has been
A museum it should be
To kindle the memory
Of one such as thee

Eighty-five thousand
Dollars each year
To keep the doors open
To keep your life story here
Baltimore has paid
Year in and year out
Pride for a resident
Who stood tall and stout

With your Aunt Maria Clemm
In that house on that street
You lived for a spell
Through winter snows, summer heat

The many engravings
On the second floor today
Depict THE RAVEN
Art by Gustav Doré

And your sad obituary
When Griswold dismissed you
Hangs on a wall
It's on display too

With Virginia your cousin
You lived in that place
A beautiful child
An angelic face

She was just ten
You were twenty-three
And three years later
Married you would be

Then off to Richmond
To edit much lore
Twenty-six-years
Before the Civil War

The path you then took
And the price that you paid
Soon became famous
What a name that you made

One thousand brilliant pages
Of lyric poems, tales of the tomb
Grotesque murders, creeping horrors
Flights of fancy from the writer's loom

Detective tales, the first in history
Science fiction never seen before
Visions of heaven, even angels
Riches of literature for evermore!

Some years later back in Baltimore
In an alley dismal and dark
Someone discovered you'd fallen
The setting, chilling and stark

For a week you had been missing
Yet as you lay in your hospital bed
No foul play did you report
Despite suspicions quite widespread

For a few days you did struggle
To cling to your sorrowful life
A master of literary achievements
Yet a life of so much strife

To the cemetery they swiftly took you
And then they buried you so deep
At your funeral, scant attention
Five or six people and hardly a peep

THE POE HOUSE IN BALTIMORE

Your fame, your name, already tarnished
To forget you, Baltimore thought it best
That barely a stone should mark your gravesite
Where you began your eternal rest

Many years passed before they erected
A suitable tomb, not at all so plain
At your gravesite in old Baltimore
Where reside your earthly remains

Were you not always an orphan?
In more ways than merely one?
Now an orphan to your city
That never accepted you as a true son

Honoring baseball's home-run champion
At Babe Ruth's Baltimore home
The city spends fifty-five thousand dollars
An annual expense, not a loan

But for Poe eighty-five thousand dollars
Has become a burden, such a steep price
Before the city could expend it
They had to consider – had to think twice

So the museum for Ruth stays
The museum for Poe goes
City budgets are tight
Everyone knows

13. FORRY

(*Note to the Reader:* This is another true poem and portrait, this time about my mentor in film and realms of imagination, Forrest J Ackerman, or Forry. The lack of a period after his middle initial is not a typographical error. By deliberate choice he never used one. He was known at times as 4E, 4SJ, FJA, Dr. Acula and Mr. Science-Fiction. He was famous as the original editor of Famous Monsters of Filmland Magazine, the world's first monster magazine that revealed the secrets of Hollywood special effects to a young generation. He coined the term Sci-Fi. He was an atheist who didn't believe in a life hereafter. After he passed, strange things happened to me and several others of his close friends – things that gave us the distinct impression that we were hearing from him from another realm. This propelled my production of the feature documentary film, THE LIFE AFTER DEATH PROJECT. Noted author Richard Matheson states, for the record, that he believes after Forry passed, Forry decided to do something practical to let me and others know he had been mistake about there being no "hereafter.")

Forrest J Ackerman, one of my Literary and Cinematic Mentors.

FORRY

It was a false December
A night lacking wisps of cold
He had lived life to the fullest
And he creaked like one too old

Ninety-two, that seemed a splendid age
For farewells to one and all
But he had hoped to reach a hundred
Before the darkness would fall

Immersed in thoughts of his dear mate
Wendayne, deceased eighteen years
Devotion to her beckoned him still
But no longer any tears

Time left no clue as it marched on
No hint, no answer known
How dear friends would face his loss
But his zest for life had flown

I do remember how I felt
When news of his death was heard
He was like my dearest uncle
My loneliness painfully stirred

It was a false December
When he chose to leave this world
Certain there was no other
No flags to be unfurled

His grave at Forrest Lawn
Is not beneath the ground
In a wall it is, at shoulder's height
That's where his bones are found

He didn't expect to meet his Maker
Forry was convinced that he had none
That from evolution we all sprang by chance
Like all other beings beneath the sun
He was sure he would not remember
Ever having been alive
That no pearly gates would greet him
At no heaven would he arrive
He was certain he'd be forgotten
By the world in which he grew
Oh, perhaps some might recall him
But only for a year or two
And when all those he had called his friend
Were themselves gone from this Earth
What purpose then, what reason given
For the fact of his own birth?

But those who knew him loved him still
More than he would ever guess
They would not release their grasp on him
As he went to his long rest

And as for things that came to pass
Imagine my shock and surprise
When events that no one could explain
Made it impossible to think otherwise
Than that from Beyond, Forry reached out
To contact many a friend
And I was one who heard from him
The messages did not end
I became certain of my conclusion
He was such an excellent host
The things he did to awaken me
Were like games played by a ghost

I never knew when he would come
Into my world once more
But come he did, repeatedly
Gliding through every door

FORRY

The messages that he left for me
Were odd and strange, that's true
But I'm not alone among his friends
He favors some that he knew

He haunts me now, and I welcome him
My devotion remains quite steady
His other friends, they feel the same
For his visits we are ready

And as for his sense of humor
Don't claim that now there is none
We expect that all his messages
Will convey an original pun

What did he find on the Other Side?
Does he still wear Lugosi's cape?
And how can we discern his form?
Can we ever know his shape?

Will he ever appear to say hello
To make it clear he has returned?
And how can he pass from there to here?
Without ever being discerned?

Is he telling us that life goes on
In another world not far?
Is he announcing that his spirit lives
Like the light from a distant star?

Is he telling us to fear not death?
To abandon our thoughts of terror?
And to announce that all his many doubts
Were in fact his greatest error?

My son, Scott M. Davids at age ten with "Uncle Forry." Scott grew up to be a master Hollywood special effects supervisor, as well as an award-winning co-producer/editor of my film THE SCI-FI BOYS, *streaming on Netflix from March 2012 to March 2015.*

Hollace Davids (left), Forrest J Ackerman (center) and I (right) bask at the premiere of THE SCI-FI BOYS *(2006) at the Hollywood Egyptian Theater, where a large tribute for Forry was held almost exactly three years later.*

The DVD cover of THE SCI-FI BOYS, *painting by Basil Gogos.*

I'm with Forrest J Ackerman (right) signing autographs at San Diego Comic-Con celebrating the Universal Pictures Home Entertainment release of THE SCI-FI BOYS *the summer of 2006. Forry was then 89.*

Hollace Davids (left) and I receive the Saturn Award from the Academy of Science-Fiction, Fantasy and Horror for Best DVD of 2006 for THE SCI-FI BOYS

Final Photo taken of me with Forrest J Ackerman (Oct. 31, 2008), who passed away at two minutes to midnight, December 4, 2008.

Key Art for THE LIFE AFTER DEATH PROJECT showing Forrest J Ackerman with Bela Lugosi's "Dracula," ring for my film that deals with a scientific investigation of apparent messages from Forry over a several year period following his passing. The painting, made four years before he died, predicts the exact time of his death on the clock.

14. AUNT TESS AND THE HAUNTING

The haunt of course
Receives it force
In all renditions
From repetitions

You notice something
Somewhat ajar
As if a message
From someone afar

An object out of place
With no obvious reason
It could happen any day
In any season

But this is February, cold and mean
Nasty drafts and things unseen
Make dishes rattle and a bottle roll
A bell will toll, you spy the Indian bowl

A small baked bowl of Indian craft
From ancient days, an era passed
A gift from an aunt who you do cherish
Part Indian blood, traditions to relish

The bowl has no legs to walk around
But it moved from the table without a sound
It's now on the floor on planks of wood
You try not to notice but you know you should

You pass it off
As just a fluke
Lest friends and family
Judge you a kook

A shoulder shrug
Achieves your aim
Of dismissing the thing
Without placing blame

And then again
The object moves
To an unlikely place
That you did not choose

You inquire to all but it's no use
No one came by, no prankster is loose
Again you place the bowl right back
On the wall behind it there is a crack

And above the crack there hangs a photo
Your aunt from off in Minnesota
You give it a glance, you are all alone
And suddenly the ringing of a phone

It's your aunt who's called
You are not charmed
You have never heard
A voice so alarmed

She tells of a relic in her home
A carving with a mind of its own
A sculpture that moves without a touch
It's frightened her very much

You do your best to bring her calm
You dismiss her state of extreme alarm
You insist that all things anthropological
Have an explanation that's quite logical

But do you believe it, are you sure?
The photo of your aunt acts like a lure
You stand before it to look and stare
It now has a stain that wasn't there

AUNT TESS AND THE HAUNTING

The stain is shaped strangely like a "T"
Your aunt's name is Tess, how can this be?
You try to sleep to no avail
You toss and turn, it starts to hail

The hail is loud, no trifling matter
A howling wind, your window shatters
The wind blows through the window broken
It's like mystical words cryptically spoken

Tess and death are the words you hear
Those words fill you with much fear
A portent dark, Tess you must phone
The phone won't work, and you're all alone

It was Tess who gave you that bowl so strange
It was Tess who in your boyhood would rearrange
Your conviction of what can and cannot be
Your knowledge of things the eye can't see

Aunt Tess opened so many hidden doors
Of mind over matter, worlds to explore
To teach you there are things you cannot see
Don't be too sure of what cannot be

You slam the bedroom door to block
The speaking wind, your door you lock
You snuggle under covers thick
The photo of Aunt Tess falls like a brick

It strikes the tail of Truffle your cat
Truffle screeches loud and does attack
This gentle cat who you love to catch
Shrieks and with claws your arm does scratch

There's a streak of blood, you feel the pain
The hail outside now is pounding rain
You treat the wound, you scold the cat
You fall asleep, you dream of a rat

In darkness cold with blankets firm
At your naked feet, you sense a worm
Crawling up your ankle, the blankets ruffle
You sweat with fear, but it's only Truffle

As dawn's light ripples across the rug
Someone at the base of your bed does tug
Your blankets hard, a sudden force
But there is no one there, of course

You reach for the phone and again will try
But at that instant it rings, your ears don't lie
From Minnesota Uncle William calls
To tell you Tess took two tragic falls

The first from her bed, when a rat scampered by
The second down the stairs, you hear Will cry
Aunt Tess has died, but of course you knew
Yesterday's signs alerted you

No hail nor rain nor wind that speaks
No falling photos or floors that creak
A pale sun is out and all is calm
Into your mind come the words of a Psalm

Yay though I walk through
The shadow of the Valley of Death
And standing there fearful
You try to catch your breath

But the bedroom door
That you locked at night
Has given you
Yet one more fright

It is unlocked now
That's no delusion
You did not unlock it
That's no illusion

And the Indian bowl
Is no longer there
A doorway through time
It did tear

The tears come slowly for dear Aunt Tess
She was like a mother in times of stress
Her death hits hard with such cruel force
And all the more from the haunting, of course

Now you never forget to look for signs
They are everywhere within our minds
They speak to us, and strange things are shown
Especially when we are all alone

15. RAY HARRYHAUSEN, THE HERO

(*Note to the Reader*: This is another true-to-life poem, a tribute to one of my inspirations and mentors, to whom I was introduced by Forrest J Ackerman. The photo below was taken at Forry's Ackermansion, an 18-room home filled with science-fiction, horror and fantasy film memorabilia. This was the night when I first met Ray Harryhausen, one of the greatest cinema visionaries and special effects pioneers.)

Ray Harryhausen (left) with one of his greatest admirers - me! (1986)

RAY HARRYHAUSEN, THE HERO

Hooray for Ray Harryhausen
My hero since age eight
He enticed me to believe in monsters
For his movies I could not wait

My awe for him commenced
On Sinbad's voyage number seven
Bernard Hermann's score at the credits
No denying that I was in heaven

I could not believe my eyes
Seeing the stone face above the cave
I gripped my seat and my popcorn bag
At the cliffs of Colossa, such huge waves

The roar of the Cyclops reached my ears
Before it lurched into the light
The magician fled with the magic lamp
Sokurah running in fright

And then my young eyes did behold
A sight no boy should have seen
A gigantic one-eyed monster
Cloven hoofs, a snarl, quite mean

The magician rubbed that lamp and said
Magic words of which I'm fond
Green smoke poured out from the magic lamp
From the land beyond Beyond

And then the genie did appear
A boy very much like me
He walled that wicked Cyclops in
That was his destiny

The genie's moment on the screen
As my candy spilled to the floor
Transformed this boy, making him dream
Vast dreams forevermore

At last I pried some secrets
Hidden mysteries that I did crave
From Famous Monsters magazine
About how Sinbad's monsters were made

Those huge monsters were not tall at all
More like dolls clutched by a child
Ray Harryhausen towered over them
In real life, they were deceptively mild

Ray's creatures were small puppets
No strings, no hand inside
It was called stop-motion animation
Harryhausen's wild ride

The little lifeless puppets
He adjusted one frame at a time
Twenty-four frames each second
When completed, it was sublime

Every film took him a year in the dark
That's what he finally revealed
But all the rest of the secrets
He very deliberately concealed

The next Ray Harryhausen I ached to be
A lifestyle certain to be groovy
But thousands of other kids were the same
Wanting to make a monster movie

A long list of monster kids
Lived for their cinema dreams
But could a million Ray Harryhausens
Work in future special effects teams?

Look at the credits of any movie
That answer: a resounding yes
So many digital effects artists on every film
Simply amazing, I must confess

RAY HARRYHAUSEN, THE HERO

But it was not always so
And that's what I want you to know
In a garage it began with one lonely man
A man who had hardly a single fan

He sculpted creatures from his dreams
He proved that all was not as it seems
He made monsters tower above us all
In the last reel, the beast would take a fall

So many beasts, I can hardly name them
But I love them all so I shall try
San Francisco destroyed by an Octopus
Giant tentacles reaching into the sky

Another beast, from twenty thousand fathoms
Crept to a lighthouse from undersea caverns
Mighty Joe Young, he was a dynamo
Orphanage burning, how it did glow

Robot men from the depths of space
Targeted their rays at the human race
The Ymir from Venus, bigger than a whale
The Colosseum's walls it did scale

Sinbad's men, they found time and again
Creatures confronting them, nine or ten
Cyclops, dragon, skeletons, too
Snake woman, giant rocs, what would they do?

Spears and lances, cannons and tanks
They killed those monsters, got no thanks
Then there was Mysterious Island's brew
A giant crab, made quite a stew

Bees bigger than a house walled people in
A giant dodo bird – I leaped out of my skin
Slay a giant crocodile? Gulliver did
But from a giant squirrel he ran and hid

Jason and the Argonauts seeking the Golden Fleece
An army of skeletons gave them no peace
A hissing hydra, seven heads on long necks
It turned all my friends into nervous wrecks

Gwangi the tyrannosaur in a western town
Cowboys with ropes finally brought him down
And what did the first men in the moon behold?
A giant moon cow, that's what they told

And then finally on Mount Olympus
Zeus and all his Titans clashed
While Perseus fought the Medussa
All his hopes were nearly dashed

The Medussa's head of snakes
At Perseus snarled and leered
Only glance at her through a mirror
She is to be quite feared

For if you gaze at her straight on
You won't even have time to moan
Her green eyes will instantly
Turn you into stone

At long last the Motion Picture Academy
Finally called out Ray's long name
Up the aisle to much applause
For his Oscar he proudly came

The late Willis O'Brien roared like King Kong
And George Pal from Beyond also cheered
Ray's mentors all applauded his films
To those films they were endeared

Beloved Master, Ray Harryhausen
Esteemed artist that you are
Now even on Hollywood Boulevard
At last you have a star!

Three old friends and giants of science-fiction and fantasy cinema and literature – Forrest J Ackerman (left), Ray Bradbury (center), Ray Harryhausen (right).

16. THE FUTURE

One million years from now or more
What will the future have in store?
Now I don't mean to leave you scowling
But dinosaurs may again be prowling

Cities? Perhaps no longer allowed
The sun? Behind a permanent cloud?
Mankind's home? Maybe tunnel and cave
For daylight will people desperately crave?

The oceans then may all turn dry
The trees all gone, I don't know why
Is there a God of vengeance waiting
To bring fierce storms never abating?

Volcanoes spewing lava hot
No more earthquakes? I think not
The ground will shake, the moon will quake
Can we retrace all our mistakes?

But it was never mankind's fault
That space unleashed from its vault
A comet fast, an asteroid fierce
Which suddenly our atmosphere pierced

It struck the Earth with such great force
Both plague and dust then ruled, of course
Just like sixty-five million years ago
When life was nearly erased, yes we know

Another Earth we tried to find
While still there was remaining time
To a new world in space we could have sailed
And there a brand new flag unveiled

THE FUTURE

Beginning life again – making life anew
Wasn't that our destiny to do?
But in our time we shunned the riddle
Of how to fly toward galaxy's middle

We ended our visits to the moon
Ceased exploration much too soon
A man on Mars – not meant to be
We ran from the cosmic mystery

And NASA's reach, it was curtailed
No longer in orbit, the shuttle failed
With solar flares, satellites will not function
We arrived at the final junction

No money for peace, no money for space
No striving to save our whole human race
No thought for a future to come one day
On the ravaged Earth, we did stay

17. JOHN HUSTON AND THE MEAT MAN

(Note to the Reader: This poem is autobiographical, about my adventures with John Huston, the extraordinary actor/director, in Mexico in the town of Puerto Vallarta. John Huston's contributions to the history of cinema fill many books. He will always be remembered for the films he directed that starred Humphrey Bogart, including THE MALTESE FALCON and THE AFRICAN QUEEN – and for films such as THE MAN WHO WOULD BE KING and PRIZZI'S HONOR. His daughter Angelica is a famous actress.

When I first found employment in the entertainment industry, I worked for John Huston's agent, Paul Kohner, known as The Magician of Sunset Boulevard. My official job: I read screenplays submitted for Kohner's famous clients, such as Charles Bronson and John Huston, and I wrote synopses and recommendations. My unofficial job: I was John Huston's meat man. That meant that I was in essence a delivery man accompanying American steaks that were shipped on an airplane from Los Angeles to Puerto Vallarta. The steaks ended up at feasts at the home where John Huston stayed for years, a house called Casa Kimberly that was two houses, actually, connected by a bridge. One house was the home of actress Elizabeth Taylor and the other was the home of her husband, Richard Burton. The house was on long-term loan to John Huston, and Casa Kimberly was my destination.)

There is a town square in Mexico
With a statue of a man you'd want to know
Puerto Vallarta, tranquil, muggy beach town
John Huston, boots planted on muddy ground

A contemplative expression, wisdom showing
A far off look, eyes all-knowing
Of life's many pains and pleasures too
A sense of command and duty true

JOHN HUSTON AND THE MEAT MAN

Nearby, the rustic footbridge of wood
Crossing the Rio Cuale, where he once stood
Many a bright day and challenging night
Carrying on his extraordinary fight

Not a fight of war or insurrection
Nor a religious war with benediction
John Huston, film master now deceased
Made cinema classics, and he held many feasts

Son of Walter Huston, actor extraordinaire
John Huston inspired people everywhere
No matter where he went, like a quiet leader
Souls regarded him as a wise, great teacher

The films he made, one after the next
Came like strong waves at the peak of a crest
He directed almost fifty, and that's a fact
And in more than fifty, he also did act

And yet a crusty and rustic man was he
Like Hemingway, a man destiny
With a cigarette, beer and steak rather rare
Leathery skin, white beard, ruffled hair

In nineteen sixty-four to this jungle he came
A man determined, with so much fame
He discovered Puerto Vallarta sleeping
And Mismaloya's muddy hillsides seeping

In jungle khakis he arrived, an awesome sight
With film crew, cameras and even lights
Firm voice that shaped in even tones
Every moment into triumph, his focus honed

It was a place where electricity was scarce
Where large lizards lived but were not fierce
And surrounded by rich flora and fauna
He filmed: THE NIGHT OF THE IGUANA

His star Richard Burton was there
Shakespearian actor who would anything dare
Local Mexicans tried to glimpse, near and far
The co-stars Ava Gardner and Deborah Kerr

Based on a Tennessee Williams play
That black and white movie had its day
It came and then went but was first rate
John Huston in that jungle found his fate

Puerto Vallarta with its ocean inviting
Captured his heart, the land was exciting
He brought to the town purpose and fame
The lush paradise was never the same

You are wondering how this great man I knew
The story's memorable and is all true
In nineteen seventy-six, I had a role to play
In his life when I was sent Mexico way

John Huston had directed
THE MAN WHO WOULD BE KING
And my boss, the esteemed Paul Kohner
Many scripts to his agency did bring

John Huston's agent, Paul Kohner
All the deals did make
On those deals for John Huston
Never a mistake

A stack of scripts there was
With offers pending
And reading the scripts
My time I'd be spending

Known as the Magician
Of Sunset Boulevard
Paul Kohner wanted films
In which John Huston starred

Director John Huston on the cover of American Film Magazine.

But even better behind the camera
John Huston should be
So to his rather large office
Paul Kohner called me

I read the screenplays
To consider their potential
My opinion was one of many
I was deferential

But if a script struck me
As great beyond measure
In that knowledge
Paul Kohner took pleasure

In the stack before me
Was one that amazed
So powerful it was
It left me quite dazed

I advised Paul Kohner
Of its title that day
It was called
THE MAN WHO CAME TO PLAY

Neither of us could know at that time
That it would win Best Picture in seventy-nine
The name eventually would be changed
Into THE DEERHUNTER it was rearranged

For John Huston the screenplay was submitted
Before Michael Cimino as director was committed
Paul Kohner put that script at the top of the stack
And asked me if a passport I did lack

A passport I had from some previous travel
Said Paul Kohner: "Your weekend plans I shall unravel
To Mexico I'm sending you, you'll leave tomorrow
And on this trip, you will have no sorrow
For in Puerto Vallarta, you will stay
With my client John Huston for more than a day
You'll bring these scripts, you'll make the pitch
That one that you like could make us rich
But John Huston he has many projects in mind
He might not place this one first in line
But THE MAN WHO CAME TO PLAY
It has a nice ring
Especially to follow
THE MAN WHO WOULD BE KING"

JOHN HUSTON AND THE MEAT MAN

I thanked my boss
Meeting John Huston I'd cherish
And a few fine days in Mexico
I would relish
But more was to be told
Before I made the sprint
Paul Kohner presented me
With some fine print

"For cargo, you'll bring more than screenplays
John Huston likes his steaks certain ways
Rare is his choice, never ever well done
And he cares very much from where they do come
I know not why but he does insist
On American steaks, those are high on his list
Mexican steaks by any measure
For some odd reason do not bring him much pleasure
So steaks you will bring him, the steaks I will send
In a cooler in your luggage, but some rules we must bend
For strange laws in Mexico do not allow
Importing steak from an American cow
Do not have fear, young Paul, of breaking the law
You'll reach Mexico before the steaks thaw
And at customs we have a dear friend, very kind
His name is Pedro Padilla, and it's Pedro you'll find
Pedro will help you, without fail
Before anyone catches you and sends you to jail
John Huston, he is like a king in their town
So the steaks will slip through without even a frown"

Questions I had about this strange assignment
What if certain things were not in alignment?
What if Pedro by chance had the day off
Then wouldn't I pay a very high cost?

I had heard many rumors about Mexican jails
And I knew that they usually have very high bails
A sad fate I'd have if those steaks were detected
With a Mexican judge I might not be respected

JOHN HUSTON AND THE MEAT MAN

The steaks they crackled and sizzled and fried
Everyone praised them, it can't be denied
I was the hero who had brought the contraband
Two more Margaritas and I could hardly stand

Later that night when the guests had departed
John Huston with me a conversation started
Not about movies scripts or stories or a plot
It was about backgammon he spoke a lot

"My favorite game," he said
"But alas rarely do I win
Do you know how to play?"
He said it with an odd grin

Tipsy was I
But I spoke the honest truth:
"Backgammon goes better for me
Than baseball for Babe Ruth"

"I always play for money," said he
"But just for small stakes
Otherwise I might start
Making many mistakes
We could play for a while
Gambling just a few bucks
When I lose large sums
Well, I'd say that sucks"

And so against some very good advice
I played two games, and I won twice
John Huston said: "Son if I do say so
I'm forking over to you my last peso"

I sincerely doubted
His exaggerated claims
And I should have been suspicious
About my winning those games

"Worry not," my boss tried to assure me
If Pedro perchance at customs you don't see
Then Carlos or Ricardo or Javier
Will be there to take good care of thee"

The die was cast
My choices were few
I had my assignment
I knew what to do

Throughout the flight
My heart did beat fast
The suspense was intolerable
Would those steaks slip past?

And can you imagine my surprise
Upon landing, when before my very eyes
Pedro and Carlos and Ricardo and Javier
All of those four gentlemen were there

Like a prince I was treated
A messenger from heaven
The steaks they were counted
There were at least twenty-seven

Paul Kohner:
Agent Long
at the Top

Continued from First Page

glomerate into ever-larger agencies which, however, keep three-letter names, like mystic license plates. The lone agents grow fewer. One of the most durable and famous of them all is a tall, erect, balding, portly and courtly gentleman named Paul Kohner, who represents among others Ingmar Bergman, Liv Ullmann, Max von Sydow, John Huston, Charles Bronson, Mia Farrow, Vanessa Redgrave, Malcolm McDowell, Alec McCowen, Jan Troell of "The Emigrants" and Bo Widerberg of "Elvira Madigan." Jeanne Moreau has latterly asked Kohner to keep an eye out for something she might do here, and he acquired another new client only the other day when a casually dressed young [illegible] into his office on Sunset Blvd. and

Paul Kohner (left) with his client, John Huston (right), Los Angeles Times.

JOHN HUSTON AND THE MEAT MAN

To John Huston I was escorted in a celebrity car
But understand, from Hollywood this was far
A celebrity car in that quaint tourist town
Was a jeep with huge wheels, dirty and brown

Over unpaved roads, we jiggled and bounced
From overhead vines, the snakes almost pounced
Sights exotic and lush everywhere did I see
"Please tell me, kind sir, where you are taking me?"

My escort Jose did explain with a nod
About how in this town, John Huston was a god
But about this god's health, Jose did fret
His smoking could be deadly, that was a sure bet

For Mister Huston had not two lungs but one
One had been removed, and soon there'd be none
If he could not stop smoking all those cigars
His life would be over, no more movie stars

Jose looked to the sky, feeling some pains
He prayed we would arrive before the big rains
The rains were strong and so very intense
The roads might wash out from waters immense

The house of John Huston
Was above the street
There were two houses, in fact
And with a bridge they did meet

These houses were certainly a sight to see
They were known as Casa Kimberly
One house belonged to Richard Burton, the actor
And for Mister Burton poverty was no factor

More wealth had he than stars in the sky
And for a smile from his wife, men would die
For Elizabeth Taylor, famous as Cleopatra
Could stop your heart just by winking at you

The other house, adjoining the bridge
Perched splendidly at the edge of a ridge
Elizabeth Taylor was the owner of that one
John Huston lodged there, it got the best sun

Neither Richard Burton nor his wife
Were in town at that moment
John Huston and his entourage prepared
For much mischief to foment

Parties in the morning
More parties at night
And in the afternoon, siestas
Or boating, quite right

John Huston loved to sail
And he craved snorkeling too
With flippers and goggles
There was so much to do

But above all his hobbies
My escort did fathom
Was conning his guests
Into playing backgammon

At backgammon, John Huston
Was quite a master
And with him if you gambled
You'd lose money faster

John Huston was worth ten fortunes
A king's ransom and much more
And me on my meager salary
Well, the truth is, I was rather poor

So I was warned
To keep my wallet hidden
And if John Huston wanted to gamble
I should not do as I was bidden

One of my 1976 photos of John Huston at the Elizabeth Taylor/Richard Burton house (Casa Kimberly) in Puerto Vallarta.

My 2002 painting of the Elizabeth Taylor/Richard Burton house.

Escorted I soon was
Up the stairs crooked and cracked
My hostess Gladys Hill inquired
If there was anything that I lacked

She was a writer of
THE MAN WHO WOULD BE KING
And with John Huston she did
Literary-wise, most everything

She so kindly showed me to a room
Where I would find my bed
Everywhere, mosquito netting
To protect me, feet to head

JOHN HUSTON AND THE MEAT MAN

This room it adjoined
Elizabeth Taylor's boudoir
How exciting it was
To dream of that star

But for dreaming there was no time
Because John Huston was inquiring
About the scripts I had brought
We were all perspiring

The moment I met
This director I did admire
Many strange things
Did soon transpire

First, thank me he did
For bringing the meat
"I've had many meat men," he said.
"It is quite a treat
To have American beef
It's meat you can trust
For American steaks
I truly do lust
But planes have been late
Twice or thrice
And then what arrives
Is bad meat in melting ice
But we are in luck
The arrangements were fine
And you've brought those scripts
To me just in time
Tonight with us
You'll dine in splendor
The wine will flow
The meat we'll render
Rare or well cooked
As you may measure
And then Backgammon?
It would be my pleasure"

Backgammon, oh no!
He wanted to play
I hoped for no wagers
That would swallow my pay

I met Marisol who would frequently check
Her pet snake, curled around her neck
A confidante of Mr. Huston's was she
She read all the scripts and gave advice free

A beauty she was, but there were more
I began to guess what was in store
Margaritas were served with lots of salt
I got drunk – was it my fault?

The cooks fired up several large stoves
Then guests arrived, they came in droves
The house was soon crammed to the gills
Huge windows wide open, facing green hills

John Huston on a settee, clearly stoked
The in-crowd encircling him as he smoked
A big cigar, his most supreme pleasure
While his Margarita he drank, taking his leisure

Over John Huston, countless fawned
Puerto Vallarta had many devotees spawned
He looked content, the settee was soft
And then began his enormous cough

The cough it was like two earthquakes
Once it began rolling, there were no brakes
Eventually John Huston caught his breath
That cough of his would lead to his death

But as soon as the cough had taken a rest
His cigar he picked up, and again with great zest
He began smoking again without even a pause
As though smoking cigars was his primary cause

That night I slept well at first
But all was not as it seems
I later awoke five times
With very turbulent dreams

Nasty buzzing there was around my bed
Mosquitoes were trying to reach my head
A few holes there were in the insect net
Sweating I was, entirely wet

One bite at midnight
Two bites at three
Four bites at five
Mosquitoes were eating me

With welts when morning light was streaming
None of this was I merely dreaming
We then dined on breakfast burritos
And I munched on cheese -- and Doritos

John Huston and I held a meeting at eight
Alongside Marisol's pet snake
We discussed the scripts I'd brought, all five
And John Huston became bright and alive

He announced: I read very late last night
THE MAN WHO CAME TO PLAY
And you really think it's my good fortune
That such a screenplay has come my way?

I explained my specific point of view
The Vietnam War, through and through
Was a quagmire at best, certainly a lost bet
And such a strong analogy, Russian roulette
The soldiers they played, gambling their lives
How many would never return to their wives?
Or the lives they'd known, because of that war
A failure for America to the very core

A Photo I took of John Huston on the boat with writer Gladys Hill.

The DEERHUNTER movie
Would one day convey
That eloquent idea
In its own special way
About that pitiful
And unwinnable war
That on all of our heartstrings
Tugged and tore

"Your generation," he said, "feels anguish I see
My generation looks at this differently
It's a film for your age, perhaps, not for mine
I prefer Hemingway, he's always sublime
ACROSS THE RIVER AND INTO THE TREES
That is to be my next film I do hope
But as for this morning, let's board a boat
With this heat I can hardly cope"

So then off for snorkeling we did repair
We wore flippers and masks to prepare
A few of us sailed to Mismaloya, at a cove
And into those warm waters we all dove

Many memories I have of this life
Keen moments vanished with the tide
And of all one of the greatest was this
Snorkeling with John Huston at my side

Schools of fish swam right by us
Reflecting golden sunlight and twinkling
A manta ray went by underneath
Of dangers I had no inkling

Later back on board we all did spy
A large whale surfacing, and then diving deep
"You think that whale's large? That's a baby you sight"
And then he pointed off to our right

Farther beyond where the baby whale played
The sight I beheld, my day it made
The mother was there, floating like a barge
Compared to the baby, ten times as large

I can only assure you that this is no tale
And John Huston to me was as vast as a whale
He was hero and legend and superstar
Such a pleasure to be there, to come from afar

But on the way back
By some quirk of fate
The glory withered away
Because I took the bait

As the next feast was planned
And the talk was of salmon
John Huston suggested
A fresh round of backgammon

This followed of course
Two drinks or three
My cautious instinct
Quickly departed me

He upped the stakes
And I foolishly agreed
I dreamed of winning
Because I was in need

Our first baby would arrive
The very next year
I wished for a raise
How that would be dear
Perhaps if I directed a movie
A smash hit
Money would come
That would take care of it

So as we rolled the dice and surveyed the board
I bet a week's salary, my hopes they soared
John Huston grinned and took me up on the bet
He surely thought: behind his ears that lad's wet

When disaster struck, and I lost the game
My anxiety I simply could not tame
I bet again, to win it all back
But a skill equal to his, I did lack

It stung like a manta ray
Like a lion he roared
And then to make matters worse
It poured

Yes, I was losing more than I could save
And the rain swelled what once were calm waves
Oh how soaked I was, and I longed to be
Dry and safe in Casa Kimberly

But the waves rocked us and tossed us
And shook me until I wore a frown
There was lightning, then thunder
I was depressed, I was down

Back at Casa Kimberly for dinner
I certainly felt like no winner
Then I had a splendid fantasy vivid
About those losses that made me livid

Perhaps he would forgive that debt
And then I wouldn't have to fret
But I had no such luck
He collected every buck

A bitter lesson he did teach
Beyond your income do not reach
And if you will but wisely choose
Do not gamble more than you can lose

A year went by
Paul Kohner got me another deal
A rewrite for Carlo Ponti
Much better I did feel

It was called OPIUM
The director, Terence Young
He had directed Sean Connery
In DR. NO, James Bond number one

JOHN HUSTON AND THE MEAT MAN

Then Paul Kohner once again
Made me the Meat Man
Another trip to see John Huston
And get a great tan

So off to Puerto Vallarta again, another year
My wife accompanied me, she was so dear
For her, meeting John Huston was sweet
But at backgammon she dreamed of his defeat

She wanted to tell him that he'd been unfair
To play me for a sucker on a gambling dare
But hesitating, she said nothing of the kind
She thought twice and then decided never mind

Afterwards, John Huston I hardly knew
Until I saw him next, nineteen eighty-two
In Hollywood now, his fat cigar with an ember
He was back in the Hollywood he'd remember

I was then in need of another writing deal
And so with John Huston, an hour I did steal
We met and spoke between his coughs of thunder
How he survived I could only wonder

This fine but gruff and rough man
With skin like old leather
Spoke frankly with me
About much more than the weather

The script of his new movie
Was nearly perfect but not quite
Paul Kohner had suggested
Perhaps I could yield some insight

The movie was ANNIE
From Broadway to Hollywood
Could John Huston charm the little girl
Everyone thought would be so good?

Paul Kohner at the Paul Kohner Agency, 9169 Sunset Bd. (1976)

He talked and he smoked
Remembering those old steaks
But as far as employment for me
Sorry – no breaks

He sputtered and he coughed
Yes, more than ever before
I really and truly
Thought he was at Death's door

But what did I know?
I was indeed so young
As a director he had three more movies
Yet to come

UNDER THE VOLCANO came first
Not exactly heaven sent
Set in Mexico, it was
Steeped in alcohol and a soul's torment

Then came PRIZZI'S HONOR
Best Picture, a nomination earned
And neither Angelica nor Jack Nicholson
By the Academy was spurned
They both won for Best Supporting
As actors, what a team
John Huston, their director
Cut a fine figure, handsome and lean

And then last but not least
To cap his brilliant career
There was James Joyce's THE DEAD
Angelica's triumph; his finale, I fear

There was no curtain call
There was no more time
Nineteen eighty-seven
Was quite the end of the line

He once said with the passion of art
In his eulogy for Humphrey Bogart
"We have no reason to feel sorrow for him
Only for ourselves for having lost him"

John Huston's Meat Man
Now has no words of equal fame
However, one thing is certain
The Meat Man misses him all the same
And John Huston, to you, this I do declare
And I say this with much fanfare
Great sir, I do feel such heartache
Because we can't share… just one more steak"

"Broken Bridge Over the Rio Cuale" - My 1991 oil painting of the old footbridge that crosses the river near a park with a statue of John Huston.

I painted this Portrait of Paul Kohner in 2011.

I painted this Portrait of John Huston in 2010.

18. THE EYE OF THE MAN IN THE MOON

(*Note to the Reader*: 2011 saw a resurgence of interest in film pioneer Georges Méliès, largely as a result of the Martin Scorsese film HUGO. Méliès was the French director of many imaginative silent films that took Paris by storm in the late 1890's and early 1900's. I have long been fascinated by an unsung hero of the history of cinema who immediately preceded Méliès, who also lived in Paris: Charles-Emil Reynaud. By many measures, I believe that Reynaud should be considered the inventor of animation, preceding Thomas Edison. Using mirrors and his invention known as the praxinoscope, Reynaud amazed Paris by projecting simple movements of drawn characters such as jugglers and clowns. He became deeply depressed when French society that had adored him just as quickly forgot him, as the world developed its fascination with real cinema. His life had a tragic end.)

This image from George Méliès' A TRIP TO THE MOON was made famous to the modern world by Martin Scorsese's film HUGO.

In Hollywood, the Visual Effects Academy
For its award with its statuette does strive
To depict a rocket striking the man in the moon
In the middle of his right eye

Behind that image there is a story
One that is not well known
It is about the history of cinema
And how from a few Frenchmen it's grown

Georges Méliès and Charles-Émil Reynaud
Rivals pioneers of film but giants so tall
One stood on the shoulders of the other
And both of them took a bad fall

When news reached Émil in nineteen-oh-two
About the film A TRIP TO THE MOON
He was so flustered and upset and shocked
He tripped at the curb of the rue.

The rue, or street, was Rue Rodier
And his heart skipped several beats
In Paris, it was a crisp fall evening
He felt the pang of many defeats

He sat down by the gutter
His head in a spin
He glanced up at the moon
That moon had done him in

For Charles- Émil Reynaud
Master inventor of his age
Had created the praxinoscope
Throughout Paris, once all the rage

The fame he had known was marvelous
His reputation had spread worldwide
He was there at the dawn of cinema
And he deserved all of his pride

THE EYE OF THE MAN IN THE MOON

If you can imagine a world
Where movies had never been
That was the world Émil was born to
Inventing animation was up to him

It's true that the kinetescope
Was Thomas Edison's intention
But that was eighteen eighty-eight
A year after Émil 's invention

Images flickering before your eyes
Like a waterfall just flowing
Charles- Émil Reynaud conceived that first
And his idea began growing

First there was a metal round can
Slits cut evenly in the sides
And when it would begin to spin
Movement struck your eyes
Of pictures within the can
Aligned with flawless precision
A simple movement, repeating
It brought awe and no derision

Whether walking man or juggling clown
Or dogs leaping through some hoops
Or monkeys swinging through the trees
Or a gymnast who jumps, then stoops

A few years later Émil did expand
His invention into a theater splendid
Projection began using paintings on glass
Exactly what Émil had intended

One year later, in eighteen eighty-eight
Émil patented his Théätre Optique
THE CLOWN AND HIS DOGS amazed
Parisians found it remarkably sleek

And then in eighteen ninety-two
In the Museum Grévin in Paris, France
Émil presented Luminescent Pantomimes
People wanted to leap and dance

For thus was animation born
Painted frames, there were seven hundred
Movement, magic, characters, thrills
Everyone stared and wondered

To behold something never witnessed before
They thought: Where would this new invention go?
Could it ever get any better than that?
Could the very idea take root and grow?
And that was when Émil first knew worry
Competition arose, and he felt such stress
For the cinematographe had a potential greater
Charles-Émil Reynaud became depressed

By nineteen hundred the die was cast
Émil's praxinoscope was loved no more
Cinema had arrived to take its place
The Théätre Optique shut its door

And then nineteen-oh-two, a spectacular film
Had a premiere with great fanfare
Émil glanced at the moon in anguish
He thought of suicide but didn't dare

But Georges Méliès had usurped his fame
Georges Méliès now had the bigger name
Georges Méliès was all the rage
A TRIP TO THE MOON George Méliès made

Charles-Émil Reynaud, inventor
His last name meant fox
But Georges Méliès had outfoxed him
With a lunar movie that still today rocks

THE EYE OF THE MAN IN THE MOON

With great special effects
A wonder to behold
A rocketship's trip to the moon
So courageously bold
That ship struck the Man in the Moon
Directly in the right eye!
Émil was so jealous
He wanted to die

Émil's day had come
Émil's day had passed
He was now a has-been
Whose charm could not outlast
Inventions greater
Than the ones he made
Cinema began blossoming
Into a whole new trade!

Rather than tip his hat to Georges
Rather than plead to come aboard
To produce movies in this whole new way
Émil's sorrow turned him old and gray

In nineteen-ten he took his lifetime's work
Animation's first drawings, ever rare
And he went to a bridge overlooking the Seine
Into its waters, he did stare

The first praxinoscope was in his arms
As he thought of making a leap
His dreams now crushed, he was penniless
His fate led him to weep

That historical moment of defeat
Like Napoleon at Waterloo, he was beat
The torch of genius had now passed him by
He was at wits end and felt ready to die

Into the River Seine he did throw
His lifetime of work to the waters below
A tragedy unmeasured but no one could deny
That from Émil Reynaud, the spotlight did fly

He ended life in a state very sad
In a hospice by the banks of the Seine
In nineteen-seventeen his corpse
Joined the bones forgotten men

But sad it is that his vision was torn
By the lust for personal fame
Because in the history of the world
Charles-Émil Reynaud has a special name

Without Émil's pioneering work
Could Walt Disney or Pixar have been?
We should not forget the fact
That animation came from him

And could Émil have dreamed of a future
When billions of people worldwide
Would look at moving pictures in the dark?
Why did he surrender his pride?

Charles-Émil Reynaud we must remember
Let's give him much latitude
All of those who love the movies
Owe him a debt of gratitude

19. ZEPTEPI

(*Note to the Reader:* As executive producer and co-writer of the story of the Showtime film ROSWELL – also known as ROSWELL: THE UFO COVER-UP – I have long had an interest in evidence of involvement by intelligent extraterrestrial life in the ancient history of life on our planet. Richard Hoagland, a New York Times non-fiction best-selling author (DARK MISSION: THE SECRET HISTORY OF NASA) believes that he and his associates have identified a desert locale in the Middle East where proof of a very ancient, technological civilization on earth, has been recently secretly excavated. Hoagland's hypothesis is that the region includes ruins of flying machines from an era perhaps ten thousand years before Pharaoh Ramses the First ruled Egypt. There is a name for such an ancient time, when advanced technology may have existed on earth. That time is called Zeptepi.)

Richard Hoagland at the National Space Science Data Center in Maryland (NSSDC), on his search for ancient alien artifacts on Earth's moon

Has not all this come before?
Antiquity creaks open a long locked door
Human lives lived twice and thrice abound
Yes, Earth's secret past can be found

The ride of centuries to me does call
To reality's treasures surrounding all
The lies oft told or errors of thought
Obscure what is at no cost bought
By he who fathoms long lost years
As dreams that vanquish all man's fears

When the earth rebels with a brutal spin
Washing life clean of every sin
Is survival but a fool's illusion?
Can mankind die to all delusion?

In a dawn drowned by countless years
There were humans who cried our same tears
Who built great cities and did lord
Far above the earth as high they soared

In craft like ours with mighty wings
And machines envied by many kings
The technology vast of ancient times
So long forgotten in time's great chimes

Evidence found, it still exists
Glories burned onto cosmic lists
Look to the deserts to Egypt's west
The remains of conquests there do rest

An arrow points to the greatest proof
That renders time but a spirit aloof
So we concede the circle that is life's fate
The rise and fall, the love and hate

ZEPTEPI

There were wars then, as ruinous as any
Diehard soldiers who killed the many
To benefit the few who strove to win
Whose history speaks above the din

But the sands swept hard and covered all
Hiding evidence of man's true fall
Not from Eden's splendor, a tale
But the truth is plain, mankind did fail
To carry forward discoveries immense
On a ride to the future taut and tense
With calamity cruel, covering with sand and stones
Mankind's true riches and all men's bones

Those riches are undreamed today
But desert remnants to us do say
Thousands of years ago when planes did fly
The tanks did charge, wise men did die

They left not records on paper or stone
Nature's fury leaves us alone
Again and again as the earth does fling
Far from its path, great winds do ring

From all but the wise are hidden stories of old
The secret technology never told
But in orbit high the radar's sight
Has shined a light on man's dark night

To the west of the Nile in uninhabited land
Parched and fading in desert sand
Monuments and machines prove all I say
And now shall again see the dawn of day

Bulldozers plow the mounds of earth
Bulldozers expose this poem's true worth
Zeptepi's glory now revealed
The seal of history – at last unsealed

20. SYNCHRONICITY

(*Note to the Reader:* A term coined by the trailblazing psychiatrist Dr. Carl Jung, a synchronicity refers to a coincidence so extraordinary it seems impossible, defying odds of millions or billions to one. Synchronicities occur at specifically meaningful moments in time and space, and often the meaning and significance is perceived only by the person to whom it occurs.)

Synchronicity
How can you be?
You taunt my mind
You challenge time
You bend the rules
And make us fools
You hijack reason
In any season
The odds you defy
Without telling us why
You just appear
From everywhere
Connecting all things
The bells do ring

I once knew reality
Now it's foreign to me
Synchronicity, because of you
And all you do
To the fabric of existence
With unrelenting persistence
We think we know
And then you throw
Reason aside
Our minds have lied
Who directs you
On your course so true?

Like an arrow to the mark
Wonder you do spark
Oh, synchronicity
You make me see
That all is All, and this is That
And consciousness holds
Time's infinite folds

21. THE PATRIOT

(*Note to the Reader:* This poem is based on a concept of a specific type of synchronicity. The person telling the story was born in a house with the address 1776. The repetition of that number in various aspects of his life, juxtaposed with recurring names that relate to America's Revolutionary War of Independence, adds up to recurring synchronicities of extraordinary improbability, and yet they happen to him. My interest in synchronicities stems from the fact that I've experienced so many of them – and quite a few have involved the address of the house where I was raised, though that address was not 1776. This poem is fiction, but these kinds of experiences happen to many of us, always to our amazement and utter surprise.)

From this poem you'll figure how I suppose
That fate works its wonders to juxtapose
Unrelated events that become related
And the meaning will always be debated

Synchronicity is the word that describes
When a peculiar occurrence suddenly jives
With another that it meets in time and space
Giving new meaning to an event and place

Regardless of the skeptic's diatribes
Such events do happen, they are not lies
For richer or poorer, for better or worse
I'll show you my meaning, I'll try to be terse

First there is my name, John Hancock
And from childhood I was in shock
That in another century one shared my name
John Hancock the patriot's name was the same

THE PATRIOT

The Declaration of Independence he signed
And so that King George his name could find
He made his signature large and bold
And gained great fame, we are told

Well, other John Hancocks there surely must be
Some unknown and some part of history
So my name in itself is a small curious thing
But when you hear the rest, bells will ring

When a child I was, discovering life
My uncle raising me took a new wife
We moved to a house that was quite old
And from that house did this story unfold

No one in our family would ever speak
Of our address which was quite unique
The year of the nation's birth it be
And ever since, it has oppressed me

Because my attention has now been directed
To variations of that number, unexpected
My college dorm building was seventeen
From that alone nothing could be gleaned
But seventy-six was the number of my room
And from across the hall there came a tune

She practiced the violin by night and day
And Betsy's music in my mind did stay
It was in fact "The Star Spangled Banner"
Played on violin in every possible manner
The coincidence instilled me with some fright
Like a destiny ominous that I could not fight

Especially when I learned the surprising name
Of Betsy's new boyfriend who always came
To visit when the night was young
And "The Star Spangled Banner" he sung

His name was Ross, and a fine lad was he
And Betsy and Ross would often visit me
They would take me along for many a ride
Speaking of our nation with so much pride

I had given scant thought to freedom's gift
Though through much of our history I did sift
My parents had been citizens naturalized
For only a few years, and then they both died

Sad did I feel, a great void arose
And somehow all love in my heart froze
But I thought about heritage and conquest
That won our nation and made us The West

Nowhere in my story do I wish to brag
But remember Betsy Ross designed our flag
And the year I shall at once confess
It was the same as my childhood address

But there was more to seventeen seventy-six
When he was seventeen Ross had tried to enlist
In the Navy, and that plan gave him much bliss
But he was underage, it was a near miss

At age seventeen he applied in June
The seventh day of the sixth month
The number's endurance
I now could trust

They discovered his age
Ross was a dunce
They turned him away
And denied him at once
But 1776 followed me
Wherever I went
Like madness encroaching
And reason spent

THE PATRIOT

When I applied for a passport,
Intending to travel
Truly my sanity
Began to unravel
The passport number
Had seventeen seventy-six
I trembled and shook
Was my mind playing tricks?

Alone I set forth for London
Going by plane
And the man sitting next to me
Well, he had a strange name

His last name was Revere
His first name Saul
I noticed at once
That it rhymed with Paul

Our flight number?
It was seventy-six
And my seat number?
It was also fixed
Yes, it was seat seventeen
Right by the aisle
Oh, how I wish
That I could have cracked a smile

But my mood was dark
My trust was low
My sense of fate
Kept my mind in tow

Why could I not those numbers escape?
My name must be the cause of the recurring date!
That year of war when independence we declared
With Paul Revere's warning how much better we fared
With the Betsy Ross flag flying so high
It was the star spangled banner up in the sky

At my hotel in London I at once lost my key
Some sort of strange fog had come over me
I spoke to the manager, Francis by name
His son got me a new key and Scott was his name
Francis and Scott had provided the key
And now a new fear came over me
For Francis Scott Key had composed the verse
Of our national anthem, for better or worse

My hotel in London also connected
Because of the streets that intersected
Right where King Street and George Street meet
And I was on the third floor, now wasn't that sweet?

King George the Third had the colonies fought
Back in grade school all those facts I was taught
The war had been fierce, brutal was the fight
Our rag-tag army fought by day and night

I dreamed of John Hancock, the patriot fierce
Who the portals of the ages did pierce
To rich and poor, all defend
His mission: equality, to the end
And concepts of justice he transcended
And even British soldiers he defended
A treaty was needed when the war ended
It is said that John Hancock penned it

I awoke in a sweat, knowing not what to think
I decided that I could do with a stiff drink
My memories intense, could it be I was he?
And I'd returned with my name, beyond history?
One drink led to two and then to some more
And then I stumbled right out the door

The man in the flat at the bottom did scream
Right at my face, that man he was quite mean
He called me a bloody American, that's what he said
He declared that my type would be better off dead

THE PATRIOT

"America thinks she can push us around
You start lots of wars, so we devalue our pound
Surrendering to the colonies was our biggest mistake
We'd own you today if your troops we did break"

I defended our honor, a patriot firm
And then I spit in his face, that man was a worm
He punched me quite hard, and over I flew
I felt all alone and knew not what to do

I should never have been in London that day
Whatever possessed me to go there to stay
I boarded a bus when I should have walked
If only I had listened instead of talked

Martha who was in the hotel room next door
Tried to warn me that London was in a war
Terrorists and anarchists were all over the street
How could I know what evil I'd meet?

I boarded a bus, the number seventeen
It didn't seem real, like yet another dream
Seven people there were on the bus lower floor
With me, six on the top, then I did hear a roar

The bomb it was sudden
The blast was immense
The noise was colossal
The smoke was so dense

Synchronicity can be either enemy or friend
But when it sneaks up, your mind it will bend
It steals your reason, takes over your verse
It is the secret fabric of this universe

22. SOUL IN FLIGHT

Twice upon a midnight weary
Drearily tapping something nearly
Comprehensible yet scarcely known,
While I held a forgotten tome
Its lore intense with wonders flowing
From its pages, secrets I'd be knowing
The power of their ciphers found
A power soon spread all around

The rapping, tapping caught me napping
My soul's flurry of flight yes really happening
I flew so swiftly past hidden halls
I soared beyond all ceilings and walls

And into the sky I roamed, quite perilous
And yet my mortal body was quite fearless
For I, like a whiskered cat with wings
Have passed through a cloud, my bird soul sings

Hoping, trapping, sobbing, napping
It rains sweet milk, my tongue it's lapping
Swiftly soaring, departing Earth
I'm in another universe, I see my birth
For I am born on a rainy gray day
In September or November or maybe May
Makes no difference, don't you see
For now I'm me, and me I'll be

23. THE DISSOLUTION OF UNBLEMISHED NATURE

Dissolution
Resolution
Bones stoned from a distant ancient age

Age of the Searing Sun
Leaves undone
Memories scorching through sands of time

Time's Pollution
Revolution
Stains the purity of life unblemished

Unblemished Restitution
Read the Constitution
Justice for the death sentence of nature

Nature has no reason
In any season
To Exist
To be able
To table
Questions like "To Be or Not to Be?"
To choose to table the question, that means to Exist
Naturally

Naturally Exist by whose voice?
Do we ever have a choice?
To be born or not
In this very spot
To think and know
To put on a show
To live life free
To look and see?

See spot run
Dick and Jane
In my brain
Education for the young at heart

Heart Attack
Yackety-Yak
What's the fact?
Time flows on and we can never go back

Back to the past
Nothing will last
So what's the point?
Don't Bogart the joint
Take a toke
Then pass the smoke

Thank you, brother
Yes, indeed
We are truly
All friends in need

24. THE WHORE WITH THE BABY

The eviction notice still nailed to the wall
Kate forgot to tear it down
She tripped again on the baby's toys
So she tore the head off the clown

Mail in the box, real close to the door
She refused to glance inside
The ugly bills, like festering sores
Were eating her up alive

Cat piss in a trail across the rug
The certified mail in a pile
Her credit card with a worn out stripe
Nothing to raise a smile

The stench of dried sperm on her legs
The smell of his acrid sweat
Lottery tickets, crumpled and torn
All the wrong numbers he'd bet

Trouble he brought, nothing else
Only bleak days, never sunny
He laid her and ran, whenever he came
And now he never gave her money

The baby screamed from the next room
But for little Jane, no clean diapers
If Kate could get up she'd walk the ten steps
Then sure, she'd go and wipe her

But the stripes on her butt
Kept her on the floor
And the washer had all
The clothes that she wore

Without a stitch on
How could she stand up?
The sunlight streamed in
Stains of wine in the cup

She reached for the wine bottle
Her breasts hanging free
Tattooed witch on her shoulder
"Oh God help me see"

The bruise on her eye
Was swollen real bad
That bastard she'd trusted
Had gotten so mad

He'd beat her up good
With the baby nearby
He'd promised her dough
It was always a lie

She gulped down the wine
At least something to drink
Her life in this ghetto
Was making her think

It was okay to spank her
When it was a game
It helped pay the rent
But now nearly lame
She crawled to her feet
At the window, no shade
Never again
Did she want to be laid

And she hated her mirror
The awful reflection
She hated her name
And her skin, bad complexion

THE WHORE WITH THE BABY

The view out her window
Was seen from the street
Those men wanted a woman
To degrade a bitch in heat

Then two dudes broke in
While she was alone
Except for the baby
They yanked out the phone

Bruisers real mean
Tattooed to the nines
They snorted their brains out
Quite a few lines

The pipe was all broken
No good for a drag
Mama'd said trash the needles
Or become an old hag

She'd been raped before
Five or six times
Hard to remember
The clock never chimes

They were brutal bastards
One thinner, the other fatter
They stuck her head in a noose
What did it matter?

They choked poor Kate
And then left real soon
While Jane the baby
Cried in the next room

Kate survived
But did it matter?
She'd lost her mind
Mad as a hatter

25. A WOMAN SCORNED

The role was that of a lady in fury
A woman abused feeling injury
She walked to the center of the stage
And rehearsed her words of violent rage

She mentally prepared to pontificate
As her tongue got ready to lacerate
Her co-star who stood by in silence
And then she unleashed theatrical violence

These words of dialogue she delivered
As he bowed his head, looking withered
She knew her role, she had mastered the part
Now to express it – now to start:

She said: "Don't tell me that I can't come in
When I have come to play and win
Don't turn me out the golden door
Don't treat me like a brassy whore

"You're now the one who has it all
I was always there when you did call
I gave myself, not holding back
Not aware that morals you lack

"You're cold as ice, you're sharp as steel
You've dished out threats, each one is real
Whoever rules you now was not there
When into your soft eyes I did stare

"Not seeing the blades, the daggers bare
Trusting the man whose ring I wear
I loved your face, your hands so strong
I never did you any wrong

A WOMAN SCORNED

"In bed the many victories won
I frankly loved you for your tongue
You sent me into heaven's bliss
Without even stopping for one sweet kiss

"I'm still blind to my enemy
I don't know if it's a he or she
The one who cut me from your heart
Too late to say I just wasn't smart

"But in this life revenge there be
I refuse to let you take over me
How many have said 'I'll make you pay,
Drop to your knees, I'll have my way.'

How many have said, 'I hate you, lover,
From your cruel love I won't recover'
How many women have picked up a knife
Intent on using it to slice
The manhood tall and firm, erect
You always wanted to direct
So here's your scene, your great climax
Forget the knife, I've brought an axe"

26. EDGAR, THE INTRUDER

The raven's in the graveyard tonight
Perched on an unmarked stone
It sits in silence staring at the yellow light
It remains there all alone

The yellow light from my window shines
Coloring the deep gray night
I sense a presence and glance outside
But darkness defies my sight

Whoever comes in the night unseen
I know not who it be
No hint is there of another soul
Watching over me

And yet the tingle in my arms
And the quickness of my breath
Alert me to an intruder near
Someone who plots my death?

I spin around in the room quite fast
Glimpsing no one at all
A wisp of fog is all I see
But then I stand and stall

I hold my breath and turn on a lamp
Looking at the grandfather clock
Beside it, the shadow of someone unknown
A man in a plain dark frock

The shadow's gone in the blink of an eye
But a dog moan fills the night
A howling when there is no moon
Fills me with more than mild fright

EDGAR, THE INTRUDER

It's been twelve years since I did the deed
The crime no one discovered
I buried Lenore in the garden near
That's where her spirit hovered

I killed her with a butcher knife
Her grave's beneath the unmarked stone
The lye dissolved her flesh away
And bleached her every bone

In such a calm state the raven sits
He's come every night this week
I'm afraid to shine a flashlight
I don't want to see his beak

Last time I looked I saw some blood
Dripping from beak to claw
Whether it's the blood of man or beast
I don't know, I never saw
The attack that scratched that beak
And marred the old bird's neck
Whatever violence that stained that beak
Has made me a nervous wreck

And the raven doesn't speak at all
Except for one word Poe once wrote
We know the word, we've read the poem
I was freezing, I put on my coat

I thought back to my horrid crime
It was so long ago
I played my hand so skillfully
And Lenore's family did not know
My guilt that was hidden from their eyes
The rapid beating of my heart
And that an innocent man was put to death
For my crime – oh insanity, depart!

My alibi it was believed
But Guy Devere's was not
Lenore's brother hung him from a tree
And left his corpse to rot

Far from my mind, I had pushed all this
And pretended it was not so
I've lived a life of health and wealth
In fear of Edgar Allan Poe

And on this night, the witching hour
Approaches oh so near
I know now that his ghost has come
I'm filled with dread and fear

Oh, Edgar, take your curse away,
You mourn your lost Lenore
Surely she's up in heaven now
bereaved to her very core
As I do grieve so for her loss
My stain shall be eternal
And now I live in fear of your ghost
Which comes at times nocturnal

I know she was to marry you
But I would not let her wed
Not when I deeply loved her so
I decided I'd rather see her dead

The curtains flutter, now your ghost I see
Your torch it fills my gaze
Can that be you? Say it's not so!
This house in flames you'll raze!

The cleaver in your hand will fall
And tear deep into my chest
Your eyes are red, your laugh is cruel
Will you send me to eternal rest?

Or has hellfire reserved a place for me
Alongside the hottest coals?
Will I never see the lost Lenore
As a demon's flag unfolds?

Is my sorrow everlasting?
My mourning without end?
Can't I retract my crime
And to heaven send
My soul repentant with remorse?
But no – time shall not turn back
And destiny's will shall force
Me to suffer at the very source
Of my passionate sin
Of course

Oh Edgar Poe, you loved her so
Memories of Lenore fill you with woe
From fury, your frock is now creased
Your dreams of her have never ceased

Do not condemn me, blessed sir
Gentleman that you are
Do not tear out my heart tonight
Don't send me to a grave afar

Spectre that you are from out of time
You may make the stroke of revenge sublime
So let's add your crime to the abundant lore
Quoth the raven -- nevermore!

27. MOTHER

Appreciate your mother
Remember, you have none other
We each have only one
If you're a male she calls you son

Am I pleased she's proud of her son?
It is a privilege hard won
Mutual understanding, also hard won
But at last accomplished and well done

I have to be there for her
Whenever duty calls
I have to stand beside her
And make sure she never falls

I try to show up right on time
And make sure she is content
She's always being frugal
And on time she pays the rent

I think of her quite often
She likes it when I call
I see to it that art on her walls
Are paintings *she* chose, or none at all

I remember her on special days
Acknowledge her in extraordinary ways
Come around for cookies and a cup of tea
In front of a TV – that's where she likes to be

She always reminds me: "Comb your hair"
She offers me her favorite chair
She enjoys a good walk or sitting still
I take her to lunch; she insists on paying the bill

MOTHER

I smile when she she's proud to the core
I smile when she gives me a new chore
I smile if she says I could do more
Being a good son is never a bore

I tell her about my tough times,
But hers were surely worse
Things got bad when Dad declined
What I'll say about that shall be terse

Most of us have good years along the way
There's plenty to remember from back in the day
The family strong and happy and sure
But for Alzheimer's there is no cure

It strikes and steals all that there was
It attacks and robs all memories because
It is relentless and so terribly sad
And that's what took our sweet, dear Dad

To remember back to some great time
Is difficult to do in rhyme
You have to skirt around those years
That brought the family many tears

But all things pass, and loved ones too
We feel the grief, we feel so blue
But the sun still rises, the flowers bloom
Laughter still exists and somewhere a tune

My mother is brave
My mother is strong
In her I sense
No ounce of wrong

There are happy days
When we're together
The beach is the best place
But only in nice weather

I sometimes write too much, you know
My mother will look it over -- slow
She'll show me how to be extra terse
She'll say terse is best for every verse

She always means well
She wants the world to improve
There's too much bad news
Let the losers move
To some other state
Or city or town
Pasadena is fine
Rarely a frown

If I ever win
A Pulitzer Prize
Now that will surely
Light up her eyes

She'll praise me
And she'll say that I've done well
Now couldn't I also
Win a Nobel?

My mother, Frances Davids (left)
and my sister, Jeanie Ann Dwyer (right)

28. BY THE LIGHT OF A STAR

In the waning hour of this dreadful night
With moonlight extinguished by the trees
All that can be seen: flickers of starlight
And near-invisible flight of birds, a tease

A glance at the clock reveals no inkling
Of the sweep of time now passed
The present is its most meager measure
Meaningless, compared to what is vast

Memories fight to gain due entry
Into my consciousness that welcomes none
The oldest remembrance my soul finds lurking
Is from a departed century now done

Was I here in 1840?
In some form of body or mind?
Did I exist as another person?
Can that former life I find?

A year from the past shines gray light
At the edges of my sight I see a trace
A faint reflection in the mirror
Of a man whose features resemble my face

He used a quill, his means to ponder
Creation's depth and eternity's grace
He had a fancy for tales mysterious
Known throughout the human race

Therefore, does my sanity take flight?
To feel kinship to such a time gone by?
And why kinship with a man whom pain did visit?
Who suffered eternally and could never cry?

There were perhaps a few who loved him
His literary flair, his swagger bold
Sensitive eyes, always filled with wonder
But life's cruel dispassion did scorch and scold

His greatest moment, when he wrote THE RAVEN
A poem of remorse on a deep dark night
A night like this one, but I have no raven
To define the moment or give me fright.

This modern world, a gross deception
We take for granted the tools hard won
It is all like magic compared to old days
When all man's striving was quickly undone

Illness and plague, the major obstruction
To happiness profound in that bygone day
We died so swiftly, with agonies unending
No cures had we, such a price to pay
For being born a bit too early
For coming to life in an unfriendly time
With none of these modern miracles
Did we deserve that, what was our crime?

Chapters of our lives, then salty and bitter
Not like the present, this extraordinary game
Yet Edgar Allan Poe found words inspired
Amid failings for which he was to blame

We bowed down to the locomotive
Monster of iron, driven by steam
Devoted we were to railroads to bind us
Crossing the nation, a cherished dream

Sixty years of anguish lay before us
Before the advent of crude flight
Do you know awe, do you still sense wonder
At those wings of steel that made life bright?

BY THE LIGHT OF A STAR

Discoveries bold at last transformed
The short lives that we lived back when
Edgar succeeded at becoming a poet
With a quill in hand, before the pen

The name was Poe was short indeed
But if you think, and then try again
To follow Poe with the word "try"
It gives you poetry – that was his ken

He gave us words that flowed like lyrics
When the Raven rapped upon his door
He gave us the sweetness of perfect rhythm
His poems endure forevermore

Ten dollars a week, his usual salary
At the magazines where he slaved away
For all his poems and stories of a lifetime
Four hundred dollars, his total pay

He was impoverished, and he had nothing
He who lived with hunger, anger and cold
Yet he never surrendered until his wife died
And then at thirty-eight, he grew old

Two years afterwards, his body in a gutter
It was on a street in Baltimore
His brilliant mind lost, intoxicated
He stumbled through death's dark door

Forty sorrowful years
That was his allotment
Eighteen forty-nine his life ended
No curtain call
At the prompt, swift funeral
He had five friends
Five there were
And that was all

His three dollars and change
Could not purchase a casket
A friend purchased him one
Not built to last
A century later
They improved his tombstone
His stories and poems
Had traction vast

The thin, pale moon now slumbers deeply
A chasm of dark, two hours before light
If I could sleep, I would not write this
This sleepless night brings fearful insight

My mind still roams before my birth
When life was raw, so little mirth
I recall four years after Edgar died
In Holland a newborn baby cried

Eighteen fifty-three so proudly arrived
When newborn Vincent opened his eyes
What a strange world rose up to greet him
The preacher's son saw windmills and gray skies

Was Vincent like my long lost brother?
Or even closer yet was I?
He was a writer of letters, an old tradition
A prudent man who could never lie

He tried many ill-advised professions
Before he took up brushes to paint
He had tried to teach and tried to preach
But my friend Vincent, he was no saint

The world was heartless and ill-prepared
To accept his vision which they called perverse
His twisted shapes and vibrant colors
Won scant respect and praise was terse

BY THE LIGHT OF A STAR

And still he painted, like a madman
In the heat of day and by candlelight
Five years time, almost one thousand paintings
He sold just one, now was that right?

His brother Theo struggled to sell those paintings
An art dealer Theo was, with clients many
But Vincent van Gogh was too peculiar
To create a painting worth more than a penny

Exaggeration perhaps, for he did sell
One painting, yes, but did they pay him well?
The payment? It in no way outranks
What they thought it worth: four hundred francs

Four hundred for Edgar
Worse than a disgrace
Four hundred for Vincent
Scorned by the human race

Vincent by choice determined to die
When he pulled the trigger, he missed his heart
He coughed blood for two days and finally passed
Leaving brushes, his paint tubes and his art

Vincent was thirty-nine, Edgar's age minus one
The age of choice for the artist undone
To depart from the earth for a realm unseen
To stay a short while in that world in between

Today do you know what a van Gogh is worth?
More than almost any other painting on earth
If by chance you have fifty million to pay
You might by luck buy one if it is an off-day

Eighteen ninety he died and was buried
Putting him in the ground – now that was hurried
Suicide was disgraceful and it was a sin
There was no churchyard at all to bury him in

Nineteen forty-seven was the year I arrived
Not far from Baltimore where Edgar died
Fifty-seven years after Vincent's passing
So just like me, there are questions you're asking

I am raised from reveries
By faint light from the sun
A night of strange memories
Has left me undone
Can it really be
That I can see so far
Into the past
By the light of a star?

29. WADING IN A PHOTOGRAPH OF AUTUMN POND WATER

(*A Note to the Reader*: The following poem reflects my creative output while at Princeton University. It has little resemblance to all the other poems you have read in this collection. It is a sort of nihilistic meditation on evolution, with the thesis that the bacteria was the ultimate form of life, created billions of years ago, and all of evolution has been a downhill spin ever since. It is an inquiry into the experience of suicide, of drowning – but the drowning in the poem does not take place in a real pond. It all happens only in the mind, while staring at a photograph of a pond. The experience is a hallucination that sweeps across a lifetime from the womb to birth to death.

I received all three of Princeton University's top awards for creative writing. The first was the F. Scott Fitzgerald Prize presented by Charles Scribner's Sons Publishers for Creative Writing (for my short story THE DEATH OF SIDNEY PIP, which was also a figurative, hallucinatory death with Buddhist and psychedelic themes). The second award was the Tiger Magazine Prize for Humorous Writing, awarded for my story THE INTERRUPTED VACATION. I later adapted that story as my student film after graduating Princeton and receiving a graduate fellowship at the American Film Institute Center for Advanced Film Studies in Los Angeles. The film was given a different title from the story on which it was based: EXAMINATION. The third award, the Morris Croll Poetry Prize from Princeton, was for the poem that follows.

Although this poem doesn't represent my style of writing poetry now, I include WADING IN A PHOTOGRAPH OF AUTUMN POND WATER as part of the record of my poetic development.

What follows on the next two pages are, first, the notification of the poetry award. After that is a page with the F. Scott Fitzgerald Prize given that same year for creative writing from Princeton University and Charles Scribner's Sons Publishers.

Princeton University DEPARTMENT OF ENGLISH
MC COSH 22
PRINCETON, NEW JERSEY 08540
TELEPHONE 609-452-4060

June 5, 1968

Mr. Paul Davids
621 1915 Hall
Princeton University
Princeton, New Jersey 08540

Dear Mr. Davids:

I am happy to inform you that the Morris Croll Poetry Prize has been awarded to your poem "Wading in a Photograph of Autumn Pond Water." The judges were particularly pleased by the ambition, intelligence, and sense of order in your work. None of the judges felt that the ending of the poem is wholly successful, but all believed that the work deserves recognition. You will be sharing the award with William Reginald Gibbons, whose poem "Betrayal" is joint winner of the Croll Prize.

Please accept my personal congratulations on your award.

Sincerely yours,

G. E. Bentley

GEB:sl

THIS IS TO CERTIFY THAT

Paul J. Davids

HAS BEEN AWARDED THE

F. SCOTT FITZGERALD PRIZE

"WHICH WAS DONATED BY THE PUBLISHING FIRM, CHARLES SCRIBNER'S SONS, ORIGINAL PUBLISHERS OF THE WORKS OF MR. FITZGERALD, CLASS OF 1917, AND PRESENTED ANNUALLY IN HIS MEMORY BY THE DAILY PRINCETONIAN FOR OUTSTANDING ACHIEVEMENT IN CREATIVE WRITING BY AN UNDERGRADUATE."

ANNO

1968

Bink Noll
CHAIRMAN, THE SELECTION COMMITTEE

J Todd Simonds
UNDERGRADUATE CHAIRMAN

Fresh air and pond ripples are the promise of this month;
breathing is intoxication
and the mirror water, uncracked by tossed stones
glides across itself over and over
licking at its melting arms and legs

Unable to rise above itself
the pond burps and chirps and then lies calmly
waiting for the leaves, wafers of orange and gold
to dip beneath the surface
and know wetness on both sides

The promise of ripples eludes me, always demanding more
At first my toes are enough
then it takes a foot and an ankle
dripping droplets on the top side of the wafers
and the mirror unfolds in gentle waves

But I cannot stop
I am no longer staring at a photograph;
I have unwrinkled the edges,
and poked my head through the paper
Wading is but a tadpole;
it soon sprouts wings and swims

So,
even though my skin is sensitive to the autumn coolness
I am drawn deep into the pond
immersing myself
leaving simple waves above

Yet, why have I gone this far,
when breathing in such a place can only invite death?
Unless there is something decisive to be gained
by breathing water
and we have unanimously missed the point
all along

WADING IN A PHOTOGRAPH OF AUTUMN POND WATER

What, I ask myself, precisely is the point?
It is sharpest in the form of bacteria,
ever so fragile
yet elusively fluid

The bacteria has but one form,
like water in a glass,
but constantly changing shapes
and color

Only a circle can draw loops around itself:
thus it is more perfect than a sphere,
for it knows perfection
in the fewest possible directions

Likewise a bacteria is perfect only without a flagella,
as circular life in unity with itself.
At the appearance of the first flagella,
all the beauty is destroyed,
like a hair upon a perfect mole

Bacteria, the highest form of life,
the peak of evolution from which all else flows downhill;
that precisely
is the point

And in such a sad comedy,
the sun sits at the head of the table,
holding knife and fork
providing the bacteria its virility,
pumping thousands of yellow spermatozoa
into a scrotum
that will not grow
for one billion years

And for what purpose?
Only for the decline of the bacteria
As unicellular perfection gives way to arms and legs,
which sprout hands and feet,
fingers and toes
and finally,
fingernails and toenails

Eventually, one has nothing
but scrawny creatures,
bony and thick-skinned,
dimwitted and egocentric,
political and aesthetic,
wading in autumn ponds
or simply wading in photographs
of autumn pond water

The sun is a pompous deity, joyous but self-centered
giving principally the right to worship
and yet gives no one else to worship
And what else but such a sun would have seen things this way:
such that I,
with bones and spleen,
have no perfection to worship in myself,
and from the earth-dust,
millions of kilometers away,
must look up through vacant blueness,
blinded by the sun,
burned by my own tears

Is this communion, sun-staring through naked branches?
If the audacious sun should vomit another mighty, molten stone,
cool it with soft rain and turn it into another of me,
I would never sun-stare again
But rather I would look down,
step gracefully between pond stones,
run my fingers on the wafer-leaves,
before forgiving the sun
for having thought of such a thing

WADING IN A PHOTOGRAPH OF AUTUMN POND WATER

And yet, at this moment,
from within my kneecap and under my spine,
one path to perfection is so obvious
that it clarifies itself in bacteria,
who,
after surviving a billion centuries,
cut themselves in half each day
and double their volume

I have only one choice: to be eaten alive.
Not by man,
not into mammalian pipes and tubes,
only to be debowled and truncated,
but by bacteria, the ultimate gelatin,
which can devour me in pieces so small
that I cannot know them to be myself.

Then,
in robes so splendid, purple as pearls,
wrapped in landscapes so barren and moist,
I can regain my deity,
sacrificing this unwanted self,
abandoning all words and opinions,
pushing myself backward into soft womb-juice,
humming the tune of a cricket chorus

I walk backwards slowly, in nine steps,
giving one layer at a time to the vermin
first, the uppermost skin in thin sheets,
then the thick flesh, in pink chunks,
and finally, the blood, richly red
pumping in rhythm to the cricket songs,
each cell leaping in splendor from the veins

And so,
enshrined in pond water, pausing before breathing,
my mind is determined in beauty such as this

This time, I give more than toes and ankles to the water;
I give mouth and nostrils alike

There can be no courage in this decision
Because courage is pomposity
thick-coated boasting,
baked in callous disconcern,
wrapped up and dropped as excrement
upon some unmoved ear

In this decision, there is nothing but water
and the soul joins the water, reaching upward,
swept into the highest intoxication,
drawn once again,
into its darkest, most secret beginnings

As the water rises,
it spills in viscous droplets
down the windpipe,
bathing the tepid gray brain

And at last, in these moments,
for the first time since the days of womb-juice,
the soul speaks to itself once again.

"And you were saying?"

"Scrawny reptiles, frail upon thin limbs,
balancing badly upon the moss stone, fresh from the egg,
lungs pumping, dry in the sun heat."

"And what were you before that?"

WADING IN A PHOTOGRAPH OF AUTUMN POND WATER

"Thick fish scale, filmy jello eye,
pumping tail-fin, swishing madly against dense sea salt,
tiny head, heart ticking thin blue-blood
through porous passages."

"And before?"

"Powder scale sponge tissue, bloated with sea-water,
holding one onto the other with simple rubbery seams,
floating in paraffin,
torn by spicules."

"And what were you before that?"

"A bacteria."

"And what will you lose by drowning in autumn pond water?"

"Crackling popcorn in stiff cardboard boxes,
pouring in flakes of salt over stale Hav-a-Tampas,
dry from four days air,
still unsmoked.

Shick electric shavers plucking mole hairs
with sharp steel razors.

Dripping soap showers,
sprinkling Little Mary's water can
on grassy legs and ankle-blossoms.

Pet dogs, with groomed canine coats
Made sleek by rich egg diets.

Neon signs in red,
blue,
and yellow.

Popping sixty watt bulbs filled with black gas,
Lighting corn-on-the-cob cooking in melted butter

Perfume seeds in heavenly blue and pearly gates.
Stiff trousers,
fresh from the pressers,
with pockets full of dull coins,
rattling and jingling like Pepsi tops in a barrel."

"And who will greet you when you depart this life?"

"Earth, wrapped in brown mounds of silt,
buckled with stony ridges, rocked and riveted
with cracks and holes.

Air, dressed in vespers, twisting on coughing sprinkles,
breathing and blowing,
tucking the earth in felt blankets
and thumb-sucked corners.

Fire, churning on scorching wood,
dancing in flares and rockets,
casting deep shadows on soft earlobes,
sensitive to the warmth of mother's fingers.

Water,
bathing the stones in wetness and tenderness,
each a tear dripping down
a child's soft cheek."

"When you drown, they'll say you committed suicide."

"They'll say I was a baker's son,
grown old too soon, with coarse and comely beard

And behind their backs I traded baseball cards,
flipped coins,
and sneaked sodas during recess,
never saying my prayers
until Daddy and Mommy came into the room,
Daddy never baking on Sunday

But Daddy and I, we went pond-fishing,
catching little worms on the ends of the hooks,
all curled up and soft in our hands.

I was a coward,
always afraid to raise my fists and fight back,
always afraid of getting punched in the stomach
where it hurts the most.

But when it rained,
I'd tiptoe in the puddles with my Panda bear,
always thinking how Panda hated the water,
and how he was never dry by bedtime."

"They'll say you were no good."

"They'll say I was a mechanic,
cheap and nosy,
never listening enough to mind their business.

And, quitting school before I could shave,
read books and looked at people,
never close enough to hear them
but always knowing what they wanted."

"They'll say even more… things you wouldn't like"

"And they'll say
talk
speak
utter
whisper
and proclaim,
all in a rosy cough,
until soft-winged birds fly overhead
and drop silky white excrement
in their hands

Then they'll wipe
rub
scrape,
until it's all dried away
and their hands are as clean
as unsmoked Hav-a-Tampas

And finally, their breaths turn to gasps and chokes,
and they wriggle like snakes,
scratching their bellies on the sharp edges,
until,
lying half-naked on grassy slopes,
not even the sun will have them"

Looking into purple water
soaked through the ribs with soggy leaves,
teeth aching with acid-burned cavities,
holes torn down to the gums,
I know that the sun has made me from stone:
in porous rock is the germ of soft skin

I stand floating here before myself,
in flesh and blood,
staring into the wrinkled photograph of autumn pond water
that I hold between my fingers
the photograph in which I have drowned myself
and I have not yet awakened from the Dream

With water seeping into all of my previously protected passageways,
winding through reptiles
fish-scale
powder sponge
I am awed by myself;
for I,
living or deceased,
Am

When I was a student at college, I hitch-hiked en route from Princeton, New Jersey, to New Orleans over spring break. This photo would have been taken around the time that I wrote WADING IN A PHOTOGRAPH OF AUTUMN POND WATER, *during the height of late-1960's psychedelia.*

About the Author

Growing up in Kensington and Bethesda, Maryland, I set my sights on working in film and television by age ten when I was an amateur filmmaker (of fantasy films with dinosaurs, dragons, sea serpents and other creatures) and an avid reader of Famous Monsters of Filmland magazine. I was a young teenage winner in the magazine's amateur filmmaking contest, sponsored by editor Forrest J Ackerman, who encouraged my ambition for a career in entertainment. After graduating from Princeton University with a major in Psychology, I was one of fifteen students accepted to study on a graduate fellowship at the American Film Institute Center for Advanced Film Studies in its opening year at Greystone in Beverly Hills. Some of my fellow students were David Lynch, Terrence Malick, Caleb Deschanel, Jeremy Kagan, Matthew Robbins and Tom Rickman. While at AFI, I made a short film entitled EXAMINATION, based on a story I wrote at Princeton that won the university's Tiger Magazine Humorous Writing Award.

While on an AFI internship on a Warner Brothers film called DEALING, I met Hollace Goodman. We were strangers passing on a street in Cambridge, Massachusetts. The fact that we stopped for a moment to talk changed the course of our lives. We discovered we had gone to rival high schools and shared interests. About a year later, we were married and lived in an apartment on the beach in Marina del Rey, California.

I got my first break in film working for renowned agent Paul Kohner as his script reader. To help cover my salary, he arranged for me to work part time for director William Wyler, who needed help preparing to receive the AFI Life Achievement Award. He also got me into the WGA writing for actor/director Cornel Wilde, and Carlo Ponti and Terrence Young. I also worked for my idol, producer/director George Pal.

I helped produce the original TRANSFORMERS animated television series. My credit as Production Coordinator for Marvel Productions appears on 79 episodes of TRANSFORMERS, and I wrote some of them, too, including TF classics such as COSMIC RUST, THIEF IN THE NIGHT, CHAOS and GRIMLOCK'S NEW BRAIN.

My film credits as writer, producer and/or director include:

SHE DANCES ALONE

Showtime's ROSWELL: THE UFO COVERUP

TIMOTHY LEARY'S DEAD

STARRY NIGHT
THE ARTIST & THE SHAMAN
THE SCI-FI BOYS
JESUS IN INDIA
BEFORE WE SAY GOODBYE
...and my latest: THE LIFE AFTER DEATH PROJECT.

A few years after we were married, Hollace left her career in psychology and teaching children with learning disabilities, and she too entered the entertainment field. Over the years, she became one of Hollywood's most noted special event experts and has served as Vice-President of Columbia Pictures, Sony Pictures and TriStar Pictures, and for over fifteen years she has been Senior Vice-President of Special Projects for Universal Pictures. She handles all the premieres of Universal's major features.

THE FIRES OF PELE: MARK TWAIN'S LEGENDARY LOST JOURNAL was my first book, co-written with Hollace, with a Foreword by Stan Lee, an introduction by Forrest J Ackerman and artistic contributions from Sergio Aragones.

In the 1990's, Hollace and I co-wrote a series of STAR WARS books for Lucasfilm and Bantam/Random House, including THE GLOVE OF DARTH VADER, THE LOST CITY OF THE JEDI, ZORBA THE HUTT'S REVENGE, MISSION FROM MOUNT YODA, QUEEN OF THE EMPIRE and PROPHETS OF THE DARK SIDE. The books sold millions of copies worldwide in many languages.

In addition to writing novels and poetry and creating films, I am also an artist. I create oil paintings, pen and ink drawings, and pastels. My art has been showcased in major galleries, and you can visit my online art gallery at www.pauldavids.com

From PROFESSOR HACK HARDDRIVE'S™ POEMS, I created humorous songs, which are available on the Internet. Other of my comedy songs include YOU'RE THINNER, YOU'RE FATTER and WE LOVE YOU, WE HATE YOU, which are also included as poems in this book.

My more humorous poems up to January, 2012, appear in two other books: POEMS TO READ WHILE DRIVING ON FREEWAYS (AND OTHER WAYS TO DIE LAUGHING) and POEMS TO READ WHEN YOU'RE OUT OF WEED.

Hollace Davids and I are residents of Los Angeles and Big Bear Lake, California, and we also spend much time in Santa Fe, New Mexico and Sedona, Arizona, where I love to paint the Southwest. We have two adult children: Jordan Duvall and Scott Michael Davids.

THE CHRISTIAN SCIENCE MONITOR

Weekend Issue
Distributed Saturday-Monday 27-29, 1969

Second Section

Filmtalking: 'Sharing and developing with other filmmakers'

e 'the art of the film'

had no aim to replace university film programs with his institute's activities. He hopes to serve them. The AFI may discover, he said, some learning approaches that university and college film programs will find

atrical film producers who have agreed to finance films made here, each in the $200,000 budget category. Mr. Stevens says he'll be "disappointed" if a feature film is not under production within the next six months

The Christian Science Monitor published an article about the opening year of the American Film Institute Center for Advanced Film Studies. That's me in the center. Novelist Ken Luber is at the right and Jack Weinstein is at the left.

Hollace and I in the photo booth on Santa Monica Pier around the time of our first anniversary in 1973.

I look the role of the young cinema intellectual, in Venice, California, (1975). Two years later I would be in the Writers Guild of America and working for Paul Kohner, the Magician of Sunset Boulevard.

I'm with my mentor, Alistair MacLean, the best-selling novelist of THE GUNS OF NAVARONE. *My lengthy poem about Alistair appears in my book:* POEMS TO READ WHILE DRIVING ON FREEWAYS (AND OTHER WAYS TO DIE LAUGHING).

I'm in the Time Machine of Producer/Director George Pal, one of my cinema mentors (1986). Taken during production of Arnold Leibovit's feature documentary, THE FANTASY FILM WORLDS OF GEORGE PAL, *a wonderful tribute on which I participated. My lengthy poem about George Pal appears in my book:* RIGHT-BRAINED POEMS FOR LEFT-BRAINED PEOPLE.

I'm at the left directing a biographical feature documentary about 1960's psychedelic icon Timothy Leary. The film is called "Timothy Leary's Dead" after the lyrics of a well known song ("Legend of a Mind") by Ray Thomas of the Moody Blues

Martin Sheen is at the left, I'm in the center, and Kyle MacLachlan is at the right, during the production of the Showtime Original Movie ROSWELL. I served as executive producer and co-wrote the story.

Hollywood Foreign Press Association

Certificate of Nomination for Award

Be it known that

Roswell

was nominated for a Golden Globe Award of Merit
for Outstanding Achievement for

Best Mini-Series or Motion Picture Made for Television

This judgment being rendered with reference to Television
which have qualified for consideration by the
Hollywood Foreign Press Association during the year ending 1994

PRESIDENT

EXECUTIVE SECRETARY

Golden Globe nomination certificate for ROSWELL as Best Motion Picture for Television.

I have created rap music of some of my humorous poetry, taking on the persona I created of PROFESSOR HACK HARDDRIVE. Lyrics of some of my songs appear in my book: POEMS TO READ WHILE DRIVING ON FREEWAYS (AND OTHER WAYS TO DIE LAUGHING)

A group of the original "Sci-Fi Boys": Back row (from left) - Basil Gogos, Rick Baker, Bob Burns, Paul Jeffrey Davids; Front Row (from left) - Peter Jackson, Forrest J Ackerman

Printed in the United States of America